A Gathering of Statesmen

Ha-tchoo-tuc-knee, Snapping Turtle, a Half-breed, 1834.
Painting by George Catlin of Peter Perkins Pitchlynn
as a young man in traditional dress.
Reprinted by permission from the Smithsonian American Art Museum.
Gift of Mrs. Joseph Harrison, Jr.

A Gathering of Statesmen

Records of the Choctaw Council Meetings,
1826–1828

Peter Perkins Pitchlynn

Translated and Edited by

Marcia Haag and Henry Willis

Introduction by

Clara Sue Kidwell

University of Oklahoma Press / Norman

Library of Congress Cataloging-in-Publication Data

Pitchlynn, Peter Perkins, 1806–1881.
A gathering of statesmen: records of the Choctaw council meetings, 1826–1828 / Peter Perkins Pitchlynn; translated and edited by Marcia Haag and Henry Willis; introduction by Clara Sue Kidwell.
   p. cm.
Includes index.
ISBN 978-0-8061-4349-1 (pbk.: alk. paper)
1. Pitchlynn, Peter Perkins, 1806–1881—Diaries.
2. Choctaw Indians—History—19th century—Sources.
3. Choctaw Indians—Registers.
4 Choctaw Indians—Politics and government.
I. Title.
E99.C8P59 2013
976.004'97387—dc23
                    2012030306

The paper in this book meets the guidelines for permanence and durability of the Committee on Production Guidelines for Book Longevity of the Council on Library Resources, Inc. ∞

Copyright © 2013 by the University of Oklahoma Press, Norman, Publishing Division of the University. Manufactured in the U.S.A.

All rights reserved. No part of this publication may be reproduced, stored in a retrieval system, or transmitted, in any form or by any means, electronic, mechanical, photocopying, recording, or otherwise—except as permitted under Section 107 or 108 of the United States Copyright Act—without the prior written permission of the University of Oklahoma Press. To request permission to reproduce selections from this book, write to Permissions, University of Oklahoma Press, 2800 Venture Drive, Norman OK 73069, or email rights.oupress@ou.edu.

Contents

List of Illustrations   vii

Preface   ix

Introduction, by Clara Sue Kidwell   3

   RECORDS OF THE CHOCTAW COUNCIL MEETINGS,
                     1826–1828

Entries from August 5, 1826   /   45

    Formation of governing committees

    Rules of procedure

    Authorization of funds for a council house

June 12, 1827   /   69

    Authorization of funds for smithies and malls

    Penalties for livestock theft

    Authorization of Lighthorsemen to maintain public order

June 12, 1828   /   77

    Penalties for infanticide

    Penalties for rape

August 26, 1828   /   83

    Dissolving of previous grievances

    Policy for involuntary manslaughter

    Rescinding of kin's responsibility for others' crimes

    Policy for accidental death

    Policy for reckless manslaughter

    Inheritance laws

CONTENTS

August 27, 1828 / 99
    Marriages between whites and Choctaws
    Property rights of white husbands
    Penalties for bodily harm

August 28, 1828 / 109
    Care of livestock
    Fences, penalties for damage by livestock
    Destruction of property
    Authorization of Lighthorsemen to adjudicate crimes
    Policy for disposal of stray livestock
    Penalties for rape and false accusation of rape
    Penalties for suborning others to steal
    Penalties for lying
    Authorization of Lighthorsemen to kill criminals in line of duty

August 29, 1828 / 139
    Prohibition of marriage or relations with black slaves
    Penalties for relations with slaves
    Restriction of residence in Choctaw lands
    Authorization of the establishment of a metalworks and cotton mill
    Authorization of funds for a teacher

Index of Names / 155
Index of Topics / 159

List of Illustrations

Peter Perkins Pitchlynn, painting by George Catlin / ii
Pushmataha, Chief of Okla Falaia District, copy of painting by Charles Bird King / 12
Moshulutabi, Chief of Yakni Ahepvtvkla, also known as Okla Tvnnvp, painting by George Catlin / 13
Israel Folsom, photograph from late 1800s / 21
Facsimile of first page of Pitchlynn document / 44
Facsimile of pages 18–19 / 64
Facsimile of pages 96–97 / 141

MAPS

Choctaw districts, c. 1826 / 9
Choctaw lands in the West, 1820 / 16

Preface

IN 2006, THEN-GRADUATE STUDENT (now Doctor) Phillip Carrol Morgan was searching the Western History Collections at the University of Oklahoma for materials on nineteenth-century Choctaw writers to use in his dissertation. In the sizeable Peter Perkins Pitchlynn drawers he found a small—seven-by-four-inch—twine-bound journal, 109 pages, handwritten in Choctaw. Morgan, a Choctaw-Chickasaw, knew us from his language studies and brought us a copy of the journal, because he believed that we would be able to translate it. As Clara Sue Kidwell details in her introduction to this volume, the provenance of the journal seems to be an acquisition by the well-known collector Lester Hargrett from the estate of a descendant, Sophia Folsom Pitchlynn. Hargrett stated there were two versions of the journal, one in Choctaw and one in English, but the latter has not surfaced. Our translation is from the original Choctaw version, without reference to other materials.

Peter Pitchlynn is one of the most important figures in Choctaw history. Born in 1806, he was the son of Scottish immigrant John Pitchlynn and his Choctaw wife, Sophia Folsom. John Pitchlynn lived among the Choctaws all his life, serving as a translator and intermediary in government negotiations with the Choctaws. He saw to it that Peter was educated in the European fashion by sending him to boarding school and later to Nashville University. This education served the young man well: he quickly became an important negotiator in Choctaw tribal affairs. Eventually Peter Pitchlynn would help negotiate—bitterly—the infamous Treaty of Dancing Rabbit Creek and would travel with his people to Indian Territory (now Oklahoma). There he became, from 1864 to 1866, principal chief (often termed governor) of the newly established Choctaw Nation.

Among the many contributions that Pitchlynn made to Choctaw governance was serving as the secretary at a tribal council in 1826 that has only received scant attention from scholars. In *The Rise and Fall of the Choctaw Republic,* historian Angie Debo states: "At the same time [1826] the Council adopted a code of written laws" (48–49). Debo says no more about this code of laws. When we began to translate the first few lines of Pitchlynn's journal, we read, "The elected Council met on the fifth day of August in the year 1826." Expectantly, we continued to translate painstakingly, realizing with each page that we indeed held in our hands the Choctaws' original 1826 civil and criminal code from that council, attended by many Choctaw persons, famous and obscure.

The writing. When we examined the journal, we found it to be in reasonably good condition apart from the stained and almost unreadable cover page. The handwriting was legible and consistent, but remarkably, the spelling was that developed by Presbyterian missionary Cyrus Byington. This is important for two reasons: first, it means that Byington, who had only arrived in Mississippi and begun working on a lexicon of the Choctaw language in the early 1820s, had already influenced the existing educators and would-be literate persons to use his system. Second, since Byington's orthography is the dominant one, is used in the Choctaw Bible and the hymn book, and is the official spelling system of the modern Choctaw Nation of Oklahoma, it meant that we could read the journal's contents without having to make guesses about intended words.

PREFACE

In this volume, we have transliterated the document page by page and included Pitchlynn's strikeouts, insertions, spelling variations, mistakes, and marginalia. We have resisted editing the text, inserting only the occasional footnote for those who can read Choctaw. We perfectly understand that most readers will not in fact read Choctaw, but it is important that the text be rendered faithfully. The handwritten document is publicly available for inspection (please see the website for the Western History Collections at University of Oklahoma Libraries for additional information), and we invite all readers to examine it to more fully appreciate Pitchlynn's accomplishment. We have included three facsimile pages of the journal so readers can appreciate the handwriting and spelling.

The reader will notice that many pages contain the names of persons in attendance, some of them exceedingly well known. The first and largest meeting included 87 attendees. The handwriting does not change for any of the signatures: Pitchlynn wrote each name and then the attendee placed an × next to it. A few of the signers do not have ×'s: we interpreted this to mean that they could read and write.

The translation. The translation of 180-year-old Choctaw is a time-consuming task. It is important to point out that the Indo-European language English and the Muskogean language Choctaw have few points in common structurally. Hence, there are myriad ways that any particular passage could be translated with respect to grammatical structure. Similarly, the vocabularies of the languages do not often coincide in meaning—there are many ways to express the same thing, and many words have related meanings. There are numerous synonyms. We made an early decision to strive for the most cogent meaning, expressed the way that an English speaker would phrase it within the limits of the original text. We also chose vocabulary items that best matched our topic—legal rather than literary. This means that another translation team would inevitably express the meaning of a passage in different words and with different clause structures.

At the same time, we could not put words in Pitchlynn's mouth. At times Pitchlynn underspecifies his topic. Sometimes he repeats himself, and sometimes he is just plain vague, as if he were well acquainted with the topics he was writing about but neglected to provide any historical context. The journal gives the sense of having literally been written at the meetings, or soon afterward, without editing.

We did not give what linguists call an "interlinear gloss," a particle-by-particle translation of the Choctaw, nor did we give a close literal translation. This would have been maddening to read for those who wish to understand the content of the journal. We welcome linguists to use the text just the same, but they will need to do their own spadework.

The reader will notice that the English translation is usually much shorter than the corresponding Choctaw. This is because English has an enormous vocabulary of words with very limited and specific meanings. In particular, English has a legal vocabulary. Speakers of Choctaw form semantically complex words by putting words together with other words in phrases that "mean" what one word in English might mean. Pitchlynn did not have a native legal vocabulary—he invented terms from existing Choctaw words. Much of our translation work was taking apart these expressions in order to understand their meaning, then finding an English word that encoded that meaning.

Chahta Yakni Ahepvtukla is the place where most of the council meetings (all those after 1826) took place. *Ahepvtukla* was already being used

PREFACE

as a name at the time of the journal's writing. It is reduced from a phrase, which depending on the analysis of the formant words, is either *ahe vpvt okla* 'the people who eat potatoes' or *ahe pvta okla* 'the potato flats people'. We have elected to continue to treat this as a place-name, hence the setting is translated 'Choctaw Ahepvtukla Country'.

We are delighted that Pitchlynn used almost no borrowed English words in this journal. Later Choctaw documents from the nineteenth century include a huge (and frankly dismaying) number of terms that are directly borrowed from the English language.

The organization. The text is organized by the dates of the meetings from August 1826 through August 1828. Each date generally has several entries, each of which is ratified by the members in attendance.

Superscript numbers preceding lines help the reader find the Choctaw passage that is associated with its English translation. Footnotes to the English translation provide some clarification for passages that are a bit too spare on details to be readily understood, or define a word that is extremely broad in its possible meanings. We deliberately used great restraint in including footnotes in order to avoid leading readers to unfounded interpretations.

Using the translation. This work is intended to serve as a foundational document for scholars and as a way for any interested person to connect to the original text. We perhaps know more about, or have more opinions about, Choctaw history and law than we have expressed here. It remains for historians, anthropologists, ethnographers, and legal scholars to interpret the importance of Peter Pitchlynn's journal. We are only language experts, and we feel responsible for getting that part right.

PREFACE

We are fortunate that the noted Choctaw historian Clara Sue Kidwell has provided a detailed contextual analysis of the Choctaw people and their times. This historical introduction will help the reader situate the journal, and, we hope, appreciate its place in the development of a Choctaw legal code.

We are very proud to have been able to make this contribution to Choctaw history and language. We hope it is of use to many, especially to the Choctaw people.

MARCIA HAAG
Norman, Oklahoma

HENRY WILLIS
Moore, Oklahoma

A Gathering of Statesmen

Introduction

CLARA SUE KIDWELL

THE YEARS BETWEEN 1801 AND 1830 WERE MARKED by intense political turmoil and cultural change in the Choctaw Nation in central Mississippi. These were times of land cession treaties that ate away at the perimeters of the Choctaw Nation. They were times when Christian missionaries brought new skills and introduced new ideas: ideas about the nature of the world, social roles for men and women, animal husbandry, weaving, literacy, savagery, and civilization. The first three decades of the nineteenth century were also a critical time in the legal and constitutional development of Choctaw society, because leaders of the Nation came to appreciate that dealing with the American government was far different from the alliances and trading relationships that had shaped their interactions with French, British, and Spanish leaders in the eighteenth century.[1]

Peter Perkins Pitchlynn's journal, *Records of the Choctaw Council Meetings, 1826–1828*, whose Choctaw text and English translation constitute the body of this book, presents evidence of a significant stage in the development of a Choctaw national political identity in relationship to the American government in the early nineteenth century. Pitchlynn was one of a cadre of young men whose fathers were white traders or settlers and whose mothers were Choctaw women of prominent families.

INTRODUCTION

These marriages brought offspring like Peter who had close personal knowledge of both Choctaw and American society.

Two of the leading historians of Choctaw history in the early twentieth century have designated the period of 1826–27 as a period of "constitutional" change in the Nation. Historian David Baird, in his biography of Peter Pitchlynn, mentions a "constitutional convention," and Angie Debo describes "the constitutional change that took place in 1826 when a Council of the entire Nation adopted a system of elective Chiefs." Debo also attributed a code of written laws to this 1826 Council.[2]

The collector Lester Hargrett, whose bibliographic knowledge of primary documents on the Five Civilized Tribes was encyclopedic, provided the provenance of this Pitchlynn document. Hargrett acquired two small, bound documents bearing Pitchlynn's account of a meeting of the Choctaw Nation in 1826, one in English and one in Choctaw, from the estate of Sophia Folsom Pitchlynn in 1940. Hargrett asserts that Choctaw "organized government with written laws began in Mississippi with the adoption of a constitution August 5, 1826, by a council of the chiefs and representatives of the three districts into which the nation was divided."[3]

Another primary source reference to a Choctaw Constitution drafted in 1826 is found in the published records of the American Board of Commissioners for Foreign Missions (ABCFM). It appears as an appendix to the *Eighteenth Annual Report* of the board. Nowhere in the text does the term "constitution" appear, but the *Report* describes how "in August, a council was held, at which some principles were fixed, and adopted in the form of a written constitution."[4]

The description of the document as a "written constitution" represents the view of the ABCFM, rather than reflecting a statement by Choctaw leaders that they understood it to be a constitution. But since they knew that treaty making powers for the United States government were provided for in the United States Constitution, Choctaw leaders accepted the idea that a form of Choctaw constitutional government would help them deal with the United States government. In 1826, of course, the United States Constitution was still very much a document subject to interpretation in the courts, as it continues to be today. Nevertheless, it provided a framework for the exercise of U.S. political power. The Choctaw leadership had their own internal issues with political power as they encountered new cultural and economic influences and negotiated new boundaries with the American government.

The American Board's printed report describing the introductory paragraph of the 1826 Choctaw document shows that the reasons leaders of the Nation came together in council are similar to those that motivated the framers of the American constitution.

> The chiefs and Warriors of the different districts of the Choctaw nation, having met in general council for the purpose of taking into consideration the affairs of the nation; and of determining what measures are necessary to be adopted to promote the general welfare; having felt the evils of a want of proper regulations among themselves; and having seen the necessity of entering into some definite compact, and passing a few general laws for the government of the whole nation, have, after full deliberation and reflection agreed upon and adopted the following articles.[5]

The Choctaw council's concerns as recorded in Pitchlynn's journal are:

> That those of us here continue to not be of one mind, and we are ineffective. It is necessary for us to finally conclude that we are certainly

not effective at the things we are doing. If we continue to work and to finalize this legislation it shall be worth the time and effort of our nation. And we shall proceed to pass a few of these laws.[6]

Pitchlynn's document indicates that the Choctaws saw the need for a common basis of governance, as expressed in a written body of laws. This seems a very western concept in comparison to the Choctaw tradition of law based on family and social constraints. Comparing Pitchlynn's document with that printed in the *Eighteenth Annual Report* illuminates the different notions of constitutionality across two cultures. The readers of ABCFM's magazine, the *Missionary Herald,* would see the results of missionary efforts in the increasing civilization of the Nation that a constitution represented. The Choctaws saw a constitution as an answer to their need for political unity during the critical years of 1825 to 1830, when they were being pressured by the citizens of Mississippi and agents of the federal government to give up their Mississippi homeland and move west of the Mississippi River.

The differences between the published document in the *Eighteenth Annual Report* and this newly discovered record from a Choctaw source provide important clues to understanding the full historical context of U.S.-Choctaw relations that gives Pitchlynn's account meaning. The report in the *Missionary Herald* is a summary in more concise and polished English, clarifying some details of Choctaw governance included in Pitchlynn's document. It does not include the very important codes of laws subsequently passed in the Ahepvtukla country. But in order to understand the document in this book in its cultural context, one must first understand the origins of the historical Choctaw Nation, its forms of social organization and governance, and the forces, internal and external, to which it was adapting during this time period.

CHOCTAW ORIGINS AND HISTORY

The Choctaw Nation had occupied the central region of Mississippi from time immemorial, according to the people's own accounts. John Swanton, an ethnologist with the Bureau of American Ethnology, a branch of the Smithsonian Institution, recorded two tribal origin accounts in the early 1930s. One he took from a long account collected by Gideon Lincecum, a physician and naturalist who lived in Texas in the 1830s. According to this story, two brothers who lived far to the west awoke one morning to find the sacred pole in the center of their camp leaning toward the southeast. They took this as a spiritual sign to be followed, and the people loaded the bones of their ancestors on their backs and followed in the direction pointed by the pole every morning. They marched for uncounted days, through many green and desirable places, crossing a great river. One day, the pole stood upright near a hill in what is now northeastern Noxubee County in Mississippi. They called the hill Nanih Waiya, and it became the symbol of the Choctaw homeland ordained for them by the spirits.[7]

A second origin tradition was that the Great Spirit created the ancestors of the Choctaws out of the damp soil under the hill, and then brought them out and stacked them on its sides to dry in the sun before they went off to become the Choctaw people. Swanton finds hints of this traditional account in European sources dating from the seventeenth century.[8] The two origin stories are quite different, as were the peoples who came together to form the Choctaw Nation, which was first recognized historically by that name around 1660 or 1675.[9] Archaeological, linguistic, and historical evidence traces the origins of the Choctaw people to the coming together of three distinct groups who lived in different parts of the southeast and moved into what had previously been unoccupied territory in central Mississippi. The origin tradition of migration in the first story became widespread because movement was an integral part of people's memories. The traditional account of emergence from a mound asserts the claims of the Choctaw people to an authentic origin in their homeland and echoes the influences of a culture of Mississippian mound builders, possibly associated with the Moundville culture in what is now Alabama. This evidence comports with the origin story of Nanih Waiya.

The third group, the Six Towns people along the Chickasawhay River, were tribal people of the Gulf Coast region evidence of whose origins are found in archaeological mound sites along the Yazoo River and Natchez Bluffs. (The Six Towns people were always distinctive among the Choctaws. They wore their hair long, tattooed blue lines on their faces, flattened the heads of their infants by binding them to their cradleboards, and spoke a dialect that differed from the language spoken in the other areas of the country.)[10]

The Gulf Coast peoples also exposed the bodies of their dead on platforms until they decomposed and the bones could be buried. In historic times, this kind of burial became distinctive to the Choctaw Nation. The significance of the burial of bones is evident in the migration version of the Choctaw origin story, and the bones of the bodies exposed to the sun were collected in charnel houses and ultimately buried in mounds, which characterized southeastern tribes of the Mississippian cultural tradition.[11]

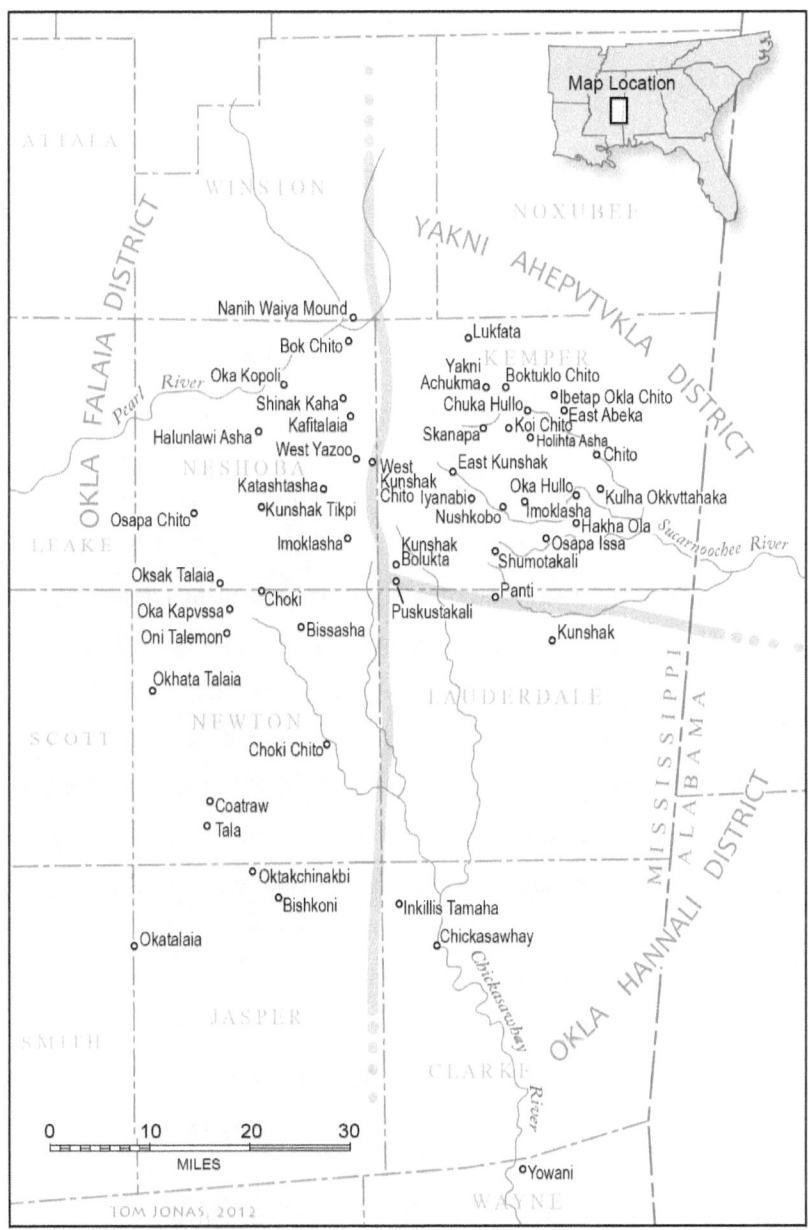

Map of the three Choctaw districts, c. 1826. This is an approximation of the district boundaries based on historical accounts (Spratt, n.d.), which places the meeting point of the districts just west and south of the village of Kunshak Bolukta. Yakni Ahepvtukla, also known by the name Okla Tvnnvup, is the Northeastern District. Adapted from Clara Sue Kidwell, *Choctaws and Missionaries, 1818–1918* (Norman: University of Oklahoma Press, 1995).

As these disparate groups came together, they did not merge entirely but formed a confederacy, which was manifest in the tripartite form of Choctaw government. It is not possible to correlate the historic geographical districts of the Choctaw Nation with the various peoples who came together in the seventeenth century to be identified as Choctaws by European explorers. By the early nineteenth century, however, the three districts had distinctive identities and leadership.[12]

H. B. Cushman was the son of Calvin Cushman, one of the missionaries from the American Board of Commissioners for Foreign Missions who established the first mission at Elliot, Mississippi, in 1818. H. B. was born at Mayhew, a mission station of the board established in Mississippi in 1821. His book, *History of the Choctaw, Chickasaw and Natchez Indians*, was based on his memories of growing up among the Choctaws. He described the districts not as geographical units but as defined by kinship. The overall organizing principle of Choctaw society was the *iksa*, or moiety, which divided the Nation into two separate kinship groups. Cushman gives their names as the Hattak I holihtah, and the Kashapa okla. Swanton gives the names as Ha-tak i^{n}hulahta and Ukla i^{n}hulata (or imoklasha).[13] The two moieties were exogamous in terms of marriage, therefore men and women had to marry outside their iksa. Each moiety carried out certain ceremonial duties toward the other, particularly in the matter of funerals, when members of the moiety of the spouse presided at the burial rites of the deceased.[14]

According to Cushman, the moieties were spread across the three residence districts of the Nation, creating six kin groups: the Haiyip tuk lo hosh (the two lakes), Hattak falaiah (the long man or men), Okla hunnali hosh (the people six), Kusha (being broken), Apela (a help), and Chik a sah ha (a Chickasaw).[15] By the early nineteenth century, the districts of the Nation were variously described by geographical markers and kinship terminology. The Western District, or Okla falaya (Cushman's Hattak falaiah, or long people), the Northeastern District (Ahepat Okla, or Potato-eating People), and the Southeastern District (Okla Hannali, or six towns people).[16] In the eighteenth century, each district had a head chief (*mingo*), a speaker who spoke for the mingo (the *taskalusa*), leading men who were heads of kinship groups, warriors, and common people, composed of women, children, and young men who had not killed a man in battle.[17]

In the early nineteenth century, the three districts had strong chiefs who were full-blood Choctaw. In the Western District the chief was Apuckshenubbee. In the Northeastern District, Mushulatubbee succeeded to the chieftainship in 1809, when his father Homastubbee died. In the Southeast, Pushmataha was chief.[18] These three men were highly respected. They appear most prominently in American history when the Shawnee leader Tecumseh traveled through Choctaw country in 1811 to bring the Nation into his great alliance against the European settlers who were rapidly overrunning tribal lands all along the east coast. At the home of Mushulatubbee, a council of all three leaders and their followers assembled, and Tecumseh delivered his message of war. Pushmataha, considered one of the most eloquent orators in a nation known for its orators, rejected the message, maintaining that the Choctaws had always been friends of the Americans and would remain so.[19]

Little is known about the life of Apuckshenubbee. Cushman reports that he was a member of the Hai-yipa-tuk-lo (Haiyip tuklo) clan, was quiet and unobtrusive, and "faithful in the discharge of his duties as chief." Gideon Lincecum, a physician and amateur naturalist, spent several years in the Choctaw Nation in the early nineteenth century

INTRODUCTION

Pushmataha, famous chief from the Okla Falaia district, in his American colonel's uniform. He was succeeded as district chief by his nephew Tvpenahumma, who was present at the 1826 council meeting. This is a copy of Charles Bird King's 1824 portrait, reprinted by permission from the Western History Collections, University of Oklahoma Libraries.

(1818–25) and became acquainted with many of its leaders. He described "Apukshinubi" as a large man, tall and bony, with a "down look" and a "superstitious" cast of mind. He was considered by people in his district as deeply intellectual, but taciturn.[20]

Mushulatubbee was the leader around whom the winds of historical controversy swirl most consistently. Lincecum described him as a handsome man, about six feet tall and "quite corpulent." He "possessed a lively, cheerful disposition, and as all fat men, was good-natured and would get drunk." According to Lincecum, Mushulatubbee was elected as principal chief of his district for many years.[21] Cushman says he was a noted chief of the Okla falaiah (Okla falaia) clan (long people), and describes him as "possessing a black, keen penetrating eye, and a lowering yet meditative brow."[22]

The district chief who has become most famous in Choctaw history during the early nineteenth century is Pushmataha, chief of the Southern

INTRODUCTION

Moshulutabi (Mushulatubbee, Moshulitubbee), Chief of Yakni Ahepvtvkla, also known as the Okla Tvnnvp district. His successor was David Folsom, who attended the 1826 council meeting. Painting by George Catlin, reprinted by permission from the Western History Collections, University of Oklahoma Libraries.

District. Pushmataha did not accede to leadership by election or family connection, as did Apuckshenubbee and Mushulatubbee. His story is much more dramatic, and attests to the element of personal charisma that often characterizes political leadership in contemporary Indian communities. What little is known of his personal history is that he was born in the clan Kin-sah-a-hi (a reed or potato, or Kunshak ahi, wild potato).[23] The date and place of his birth was probably 1764, on the banks of a river in what is now Noxubee County, Mississippi. At a Choctaw council meeting lightning split a giant oak tree at the council grounds, and Pushmataha, who had already made a reputation as a warrior and hunter, stepped out from behind the tree to assert that he had been born of its power and was to be a leader.[24] Pushmatah's power of oratory and charismatic personality overcame the uncertainties of his birth and parentage to make him the leader of the Southern District.[25] Although kin relations were important in determining Choctaw leadership, the mythical elements of Pushmataha's rise indicate that charisma and oratorical skill were recognized and were important.

The three districts and the adherence of followers to their leaders indicate the strength of this tripartite system of identity and governance in early Choctaw history. To find a common mind among these three groups within the Nation speaks to the challenge presented in the first pages of Pitchlynn's document: "We are the three districts of the Choctaw nation," and "that those of us here continue to not be of one mind, and we are ineffective" (p. 46).

The three districts had come together in council in their past history. The encounter of the Choctaws with Tecumseh was one example. The primary reason for councils in the early nineteenth century was to discuss the pressure the Choctaw Nation faced to cede its lands to the rapidly growing white population in the southeast for settlement. A series of treaties in 1801, 1803, and 1805 had ceded areas of land on the borders of what the Choctaws considered their homeland in central Mississippi.[26] They had long used the ceded areas along the lower Mississippi River and along the Black Warrior and Tombigbee Rivers bordering the current state of Alabama for hunting.

The treaties signed with representatives of the United States in the first years of the nineteenth century (1801, 1803) were ostensibly to establish boundaries between the Choctaw Nation and the United States government.[27] As the American government struggled to consolidate its geographical territory and its political jurisdiction over that territory, Indian lands became more important. The Spanish government still controlled the lands below the 31st parallel in Florida, and French traders were still influential in New Orleans. The surrender of the British and cessions of British Territory to the U.S. in the Treaty of Paris in 1783 did not

INTRODUCTION

automatically remove the treaties with other foreign governments, and Indian nations who had treaties with Spanish and British governments were still potential allies of those foreign nations. The United States had, then, to assure the allegiance of its Choctaw allies by acquiring the territories around its borders that had previously been under British or Spanish control. The councils held to negotiate these treaties made Choctaw leaders realize that the United States government negotiated on its own terms. The terms were dictated by agents of the American government, and the results were beyond the control of the Choctaws.

In 1816, the Choctaw Nation's leaders ceded lands on their eastern boundary, for which they received in payment the sum of $6,000 annually for twenty years.[28] In 1820, the Choctaws signed the Treaty of Doak's Stand. This treaty was the culmination of demands from the United States government for the cession of most of the remaining Choctaw land east of the Mississippi River in exchange for a territory west of the river, where Choctaws who wished to continue in their traditional lifestyles could move. Those who would remain in their homeland and learn how to live as "civilized and enlightened" members of society would be able to stay. The intent of the treaty of 1820 was to move the Choctaws who had not made strides to "civilization" to the western territory, and to allow those who had learned to be "civilized" to remain in Mississippi as citizens of the state. It was also designed to meet the desire of the state of Mississippi "to obtain a small part of the land belonging to said nation."[29] By whatever means necessary, the United States government was determined to open Indian lands to white settlement.

The annuity money from the Treaty of 1816 became the occasion for an important Choctaw council. The council was held in response to another new influence in the Nation—the advent of Christian missionaries. The

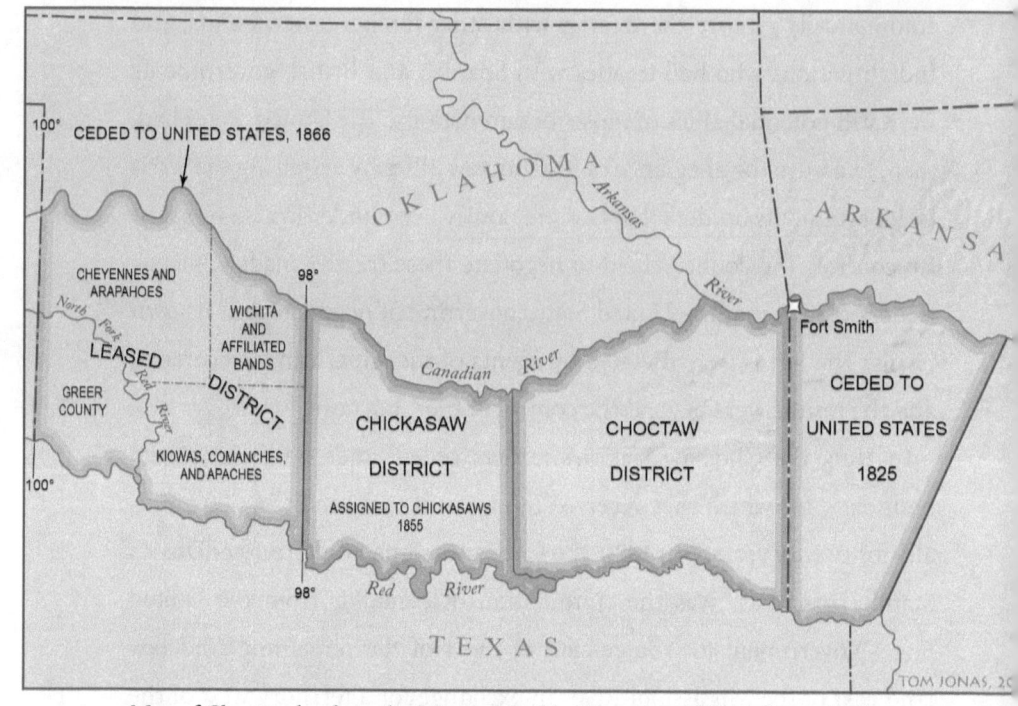

Map of Choctaw lands in the West secured by the treaty of 1820. From Angie Debo, *The Rise and Fall of the Choctaw Republic* (Norman: University of Oklahoma Press, 1934)

annuity money was to be used to support the government's efforts to civilize the Choctaws and assimilate them into American society by educating them. This intent, formalized in the Indian Civilization Fund Act of 1819, supported the desires of potential landowners to obtain Indian land, either by dealing with assimilated Indians for land or putting pressure on tribes who were considered "uncivilized" to move west.

The stress upon civilization as a force to meld the Choctaws into American society fed into a growing belief among Christians that Christianity was the key to taming the American frontier and advancing the nation's occupation of new lands. A number of Christian missionary organizations were established in the early nineteenth century, among them the American Board for Foreign Missions, which was founded in 1810. In response to various reports that Indians in the southeast were showing signs of civilization, for example, the women were spinning cotton and weaving cloth and the men were raising herds of domesticated animals, Cyrus Kingsbury, a member of the American Board, proposed a mission to the Cherokees, which was established in 1817.[30]

In the following year, Kingsbury and a missionary couple, Mr. and Mrs. Loring Williams, traveled some four hundred miles to the Choctaw Nation to start a mission there. They selected a site in the Western District near the Yalobusha River, where Levi Perry, son of a white man and a Choctaw woman and headman of the local Choctaw community, provided a house near his for them to stay in while they got established. They began the work of clearing the site of the new mission and erecting the first buildings in the spring of 1818.[31] The missionary spirit in early nineteenth-century America was supported not only by Christian organizations, but also by the federal government. In 1819 the Congress of the United States passed the Civilization Act, which provided $10,000 for the support of "Benevolent organizations" who would undertake to teach Indians to read, write, calculate, and in other ways become "civilized."[32] Although the intent was ostensibly "benevolent," the objective of civilization would also lead Indians to more settled and less nomadic lives, like their white neighbors, and open much of their lands to white settlement.

Ultimately, what Indian leaders wanted was to learn the white man's ways and how to deal with them in order to protect their own land and existence as a separate nation. If they could prove that they could live like white men on their own lands, then they would be able to preserve their ancient identity as Choctaws and their lands. What they wanted from the missionaries was not conversion to belief in a Christian god, but education for their children in order to protect their nation.

A Choctaw council of leaders of the three districts in August of 1819 was thus significant because it confirmed their support of the missionary efforts. Kingsbury spoke, and the Choctaw agent John McRae was present. The council subscribed ninety head of cattle, and one of the leaders subscribed $200 out of his district's share of the yearly annuity from the treaty of 1816, for the support of a mission school.[33]

But this action evidently did not meet with the agreement of all of those present at the council. The disagreement was actually cited in Article 8 of the subsequent 1820 treaty, which provided:

> To remove any discontent which may have arisen in the Choctaw Nation, in consequence of six thousand dollars of their annuity having been appropriated annually, for sixteen years, by some of the chiefs, for the support of their schools, the Commissioners of the United States oblige themselves, on the part of said States, to set apart an additional tract of good land, for raising a fund equal to that given

INTRODUCTION

by the said chiefs, so that the whole of the annuity may remain in the nation, and be divided amongst them. And in order that exact justice may be done to the poor and distressed of said nation, it shall be the duty of the agent to see that the wants of every deaf, dumb, blind, and distressed Indian, shall be first supplied out of said annuity and the balance equally distributed amongst every individual of said nation.[34]

It was becoming clear that the federal government was using evidence of dissension among the three districts of the Choctaw Nation as a way to impose its own form of social engineering on the Choctaws. By requiring the agent to provide for social needs and per capita distribution of funds, duties traditionally performed by chiefs, the government was depriving Choctaw leaders of management of their treaty funds.

Choctaws had long held national councils as the need arose. Common decision making among the districts was not a foreign concept, but it did not necessarily mean complete consensus. Facing the new situation of dealing with federal government and missionary influences, the district chiefs still exercised their own options when it came to the use of tribal resources, in this case the subscription of $200 by one of the three chiefs from the nation's annuity.

The concept of law was not unknown to the Choctaws. The Pitchlynn document explicitly states that the districts had always had laws. What was new were laws that applied uniformly to the whole nation and that centralized power in the hands of a single group of people.

The council of 1826 not only gave form to the Choctaw government, but also adopted a series of provisions spelling out its powers. One law provided that no single district could sell its land without the agreement of the other two, obviously a reference to the need to preserve the unity of the Nation. Another provided that the annual monetary allotment could not be used to pay off the debts of individual leaders. Other central powers of the Choctaw government would include controlling the monetary allotments to the tribe, in order to prevent "wanton, unlawful" use of the funds. Legislators were to be selected by the chiefs of the districts.

The council members recognized that their decisions represented a departure from past experience. The new laws to be passed might replace old laws, and these changes would have to be approved by the Nation as a whole.

Although the Pitchlynn journal outlines an organized form of Choctaw government with centralized power, each of the three districts still retained the ability to make its own laws. Those laws, however, were subject to approval by the national council as a whole.

A new manner of social control was needed to replace the usual Choctaw custom of kinship regulation of human social relationships, and new laws were needed in order to control behaviors introduced by whites and disapproved of by white missionaries—liquor, infanticide, and adultery. Control of livestock, which had been introduced in the Nation by white settlers, also became a source of contention and regulation.

The laws passed by Choctaw districts also regulated civil matters such as intermarriage between Choctaw citizens and white non-citizens and the relationship of Choctaw citizens and their slaves. The laws also began to define criminal behavior by prescribing punishment (usually whipping) for such things as biting off a person's ear or gouging out an eye.

Yet another significant influence was at work in the arena of Choctaw governance. That was the presence of a growing number of young Choctaw men of mixed parentage, primarily the offspring of white traders who had married Choctaw women. Because the kinship pattern in Choctaw society was descent through the mother's kinship line, the chil-

INTRODUCTION

Israel Folsom in an undated photo from the late nineteenth century. An attendee of the council meetings and the brother of David Folsom, chief of the Ahepvtvkla district, Israel Folsom became a Presbyterian minister and moved to Indian Territory during the Removal, where he became a statesman in the new Choctaw republic and a champion of education for girls. Reprinted by permission from the Western History Collections, University of Oklahoma Libraries.

INTRODUCTION

dren born of Choctaw women's relationships with non-Choctaws (white or of other tribes) were Choctaws. White men entering the Choctaw Nation in the late eighteenth century generally met the leading men of the Nation first, and often developed relationships with Choctaw women from important families. Men of such mixed parentage became increasingly influential during the nineteenth century. Nathaniel, Edmund, and Ebenezer Folsom, offspring of a Scotch Irish family in North Carolina, settled in the Choctaw Nation in the late eighteenth century. Nathaniel and Ebenezer both married Choctaw women and sired large families. According to Cushman, Nathaniel had two wives who were related to Mushulatubbee and they had twenty-four children, one of whom, David, supported the missionary efforts of the early nineteenth century, and another, Israel, who became active as a missionary himself and was also politically active in the Northeast District. [35]

The presence of mixed-blood young men in the Nation was a major factor in the political turmoil that erupted in 1825 after the death of two of the three full-blood leaders who had led the Choctaw Nation in the early 1800s. Two of the district leaders, Apuckshanubbee and Pushmataha, died in 1825, when the United States government asked for yet another cession of Choctaw land. The negotiations for a new treaty were to be held directly with Secretary of War John C. Calhoun in Washington, D.C. This treaty would adjust the boundaries of the Choctaws' western land to accommodate American citizens who had already settled there.

During the trip to Washington, Apuckshanubbee, who was in his eighties, died after either stepping off a cliff or stepping off a hotel balcony in Kentucky. Pushmataha died in a hotel in Washington in December 1824, either of pneumonia or acute alcoholism. The details of his

INTRODUCTION

death will probably never be clear, but he was buried in the congressional cemetery in Washington, where his monument is still visible. In place of Apuckshanubbee, Robert Cole was suggested by the Choctaw delegates as signer of the treaty that was concluded in 1825. Nittuckachie signed in place of Pushmataha. Moshulatubbee signed, but so did David Folsom, a son of Nathaniel Folsom and a strong supporter of the American Board missionaries.[36]

The treaty of 1825 precipitated the simmering political crisis among the three districts in the Choctaw Nation. The older generation of leadership was passing away, to be replaced by younger men who were confronting extensive social change. Part of the social change was embodied in the young men of mixed Choctaw-white parentage, including the LeFlore family, the Folsom family, and the Pitchlynn family. Their ancestors had entered the Choctaw Nation as both traders and settlers looking for free land, and they had established themselves as members of the Nation through their marriages to Choctaw women of prominent families. The LeFlore brothers also introduced cattle into the western part of the Nation.[37] John Pitchlynn, Peter Pitchlynn's father, came as a trader and married a Choctaw woman, who died. John stayed on to marry a daughter of the Folsom family, Sophia Folsom, and to become an interpreter in negotiations between Choctaw leaders and United States officials.

Mushulatubbee, as the sole remaining full-blood leader of a district, represented the only link with the Choctaw past, and he particularly felt the conflict between the past and the present. In Pushmataha's Southern District, Pushmataha's nephew Oklahoma succeeded him, but he did not have his uncle's charisma and was shortly thereafter succeeded by Nitakachi (Nitakechi, Nita Kachi, Nittakachih, Nittuckachie), another of Pushmataha's nephews.[38] In the Western District, now led by Robert

Cole, Greenwood LeFlore emerged as a leader. In the northeast, Mushulatubbee's district, David Folsom, was gaining strength as a leader.

The deaths of two important Choctaw leaders in a time when the Nation was confronted with the prospect of yet another significant land cession led to the confrontation of another a major issue. The tradition of succession of Choctaw leadership that was based on blood, family connections, and public recognition was giving way to leadership roles for mixed-blood children, whose white fathers were beginning to come to the fore in terms of political leadership. In Apuckshanubbee's district, the LeFlore family had become prominent. Louis LeFlore, a Frenchman who moved into the Western District in the late 1700s and introduced cattle there, married two Choctaw women, Nancy and Rebecca, daughters of a French trader, John Cravat, and his Choctaw wife. Although Apuckshanubbee was succeeded as district leader by Robert Cole, a mixed-blood, it was Greenwood LeFlore (Cole's nephew) who would ultimately rise to leadership in the Western District.[39]

Mushulatubbee remained the only full-blood leader of the Nation, but in his district the Folsom family was becoming increasingly prominent. David Folsom strongly supported the missionaries of the American Board, and although Mushulatubbee had been part of the general council in 1819 that subscribed support for missionary schools, he became increasingly critical of the American Board (possibly because Folsom supported it so strongly). He turned his support to the efforts of Richard Johnson, a prominent Kentucky politician and a Baptist, to establish a school in Blue Springs, Kentucky, for the education of Indian young men. Mushulatubbee pledged the entire $6,000 per year annuity from the Treaty of 1825 to support the school.[40]

INTRODUCTION

Cushman maintains that David Folsom was elected by ballot in the Northeastern District to replace Mushulatubbee under the new constitutional form of government, while LeFlore was accepted as leader in the Western District.[41] The growing influence of the Folsom family in the Northeastern District is indicated by the fact that the 1826 council at which the constitutional document was adopted was held in that district and Israel Folsom became a member of the committee that affirmed laws for the district. After a confrontation between David Folsom and Nitakachi, Nitakachi remained as the last representative of the older full-blood generation, and even his authority in his own district was challenged by Samuel Garland, Peter Pitchlynn's brother-in-law.[42]

In 1826, the political crisis in the Nation culminated in an armed confrontation. Mushulatubbee had promised the whole of the annual $6,000 annuity from the Treaty of 1825 to Johnson's new school in Kentucky. This presumption of power by one chief led to the near civil war that H. B. Cushman described vividly. In the intervening time since the treaty of 1825, Greenwood LeFlore had replaced Robert Cole as leader of the Western District. Nitakachi was recognized as leader of the Southern District. Mushulatubbee's action with regard to the annuity had offended David Folsom deeply, especially given Folsom's support of the American Board schools that were being established throughout the Choctaw nation. After the council at which Mushulatubbee refused to hand over the annuity, Folsom and LeFlore called a council, in March, to depose Mushulatubbee.[43] Greenwood LeFlore led a large body of his followers, heavily armed, to the Folsom home at the Choctaw Agency, near present-day Starkville. Mushulatubbee and Nitakachi and their followers confronted Folsom and LeFlore and their followers near

INTRODUCTION

Mushulatubbee's home. Cushman reported Folsom's full account of the incident, but the following sections represent the drama of the confrontation between the opposing forces:

> Not a word had been spoken, nor a sound of defiance uttered by either of the still advancing parties; and thus in profound silence each continued to advance until not exceeding two hundred yards intervened, when Nittakachih gave the signal for his warriors to halt, which they instantly obeyed. LeFlore and myself instantly gave the same to our men, which was as quickly obeyed. For several minutes the armies stood and gazed upon each other in profound silence. To me what minutes of indescribable suspense! . . .
>
> At this juncture of alternate hope and despair my astonishment was unbounded when I saw Nittakachih leave his men where they were standing and alone advance toward us with slow and measured steps, looking with a calm and steady gaze upon us. Every eye was upon him in a moment, as with firm and dignified steps he continued to advance until he had reached a point half way between the now wondering, but still silent, warriors; then stopped and, slowly raising his arms, he gently folded them across his breast, in calm and dignified silence, looked with fearless eyes upon me, LeFlore, and our astonished men. There he stood in his shining war-dress, the personification of calm courage and heroic daring. . . .
>
> I then resolved to go to him alone, be the consequences what they might. With emotions known only to myself, yet with a calm exterior, I started toward him with a slow but firm step, and had walked but a few paces when I observed Nittikachih's warriors silently, but steadily raising their rifles to their shoulders and bringing them to bear directly upon me.

As the two men finally confronted each other, Folsom reported their conversation, but his account of the final resolution of their declarations of friendship is important: Folsom says he "then extended my hand to him, but in a steady mechanical way that I felt committed me to nothing, for I was fully alive to the possible consequences of my every act. He took it, though the slight unmistakable pressure he returned seemed to show that he accepted it for a true sign of restored friendship, if not of absolute surrender."[44]

The incident revealed, however, the growing division between the mixed-blood faction of the Nation and the two full-blood leaders. Although the accuracy of Cushman's account, especially given its length and its secondhand source, may be questionable, the tone of Folsom's account is telling in revealing the effects of missionary activity among the Choctaws. Folsom's description of the final handshake between himself and Nitakachi is especially important, Folsom's steady, "mechanical way that I felt committed me to nothing," while Nitakachi returned a "slight unmistakable pressure" that "seemed to show that he accepted it for a true sign of restored friendship, if not of absolute surrender." It reveals the attitudes that prevailed between Choctaws of an older time and the mixed-blood leadership that was assuming positions of power.

Divisions within the Nation were deepened by the increasing pressure on the Choctaw Nation to give up all its land in Mississippi and move west of the river to the land that had been guaranteed to them by the Treaty of Doak's Stand in 1820. The divisions were also present in each of the three districts of the Nation. Mushulatubbee and David Folsom in the Northeast District were the most bitter opponents, largely over the issue of schools and because of Mushulatubbee's appropriation of the entire Choctaw annuity for 1825 to Richard Johnson's Choctaw Academy.

Cyrus Kingsbury also had plans to establish a high school where students from the American Board schools could go to continue their educations. The Treaty of 1825 held promise of funding for more schools. But just as Kingsbury was sending off his proposal for such a school to the War Department, he learned that Mushulatubbee had asked the Choctaw agent to commit the whole annuity for education and the proceeds of the sale of fifty-four sections of land in the ceded western lands to Johnson's new school.[45]

Johnson's academy competed with all the missionary schools of the American Board in the Choctaw Nation, schools of which Mushulatubbee had become increasingly critical. In the Western District, Leflore had effectively displaced Robert Cole, who had signed the Treaty of 1825 that ceded a portion of the Choctaw lands west of the Mississippi River.

The crisis of leadership precipitated by Christian influences and pressure on the Choctaw Nation for further land cessions form the historical and political context at the time Peter Pitchlynn wrote the document that is the subject of this book. The Christian influences were Methodists and the American Board of Commissioners of Foreign Missions (Presbyterian and Congregationalist). Greenwood LeFlore's wife converted to the Methodist faith under the influence of Methodist missionaries, who saw a fertile ground for conversion in the Choctaw territory, and LeFlore himself converted under his wife's influence.[46] David Folsom supported the American Board, which opposed further land cessions, ostensibly on moral grounds that it was wrong to dispossess the Indians of the rights to their territory. But the board also feared the loss of the effects of its efforts at conversion if the people were moved, and it had a significant financial investment in the mission stations and schools that it had built.⁴⁷

In 1826 Andrew Jackson and Thomas McKenney, Secretary of the Indian Office, proposed that yet another cession treaty be negotiated with the Choctaws. ⁴⁸ The incentive for the treaty came from reports that full-blood leaders were in favor of removal to the west. In fact, Mushulatubbee's replacement by Folsom's followers was a direct result of such rumors. The general perception was that mixed-bloods such as Folsom and LeFlore opposed removal, although McKenney reported a conversation with an unnamed leader (but obviously LeFlore), who told McKenney that he knew removal was inevitable but that he had been elected to oppose further cessions. The negotiations of 1826, held in November, failed to produce a new treaty, and they also demonstrated that a written system of governance and laws would not fend off the federal government's desire for Choctaw land.⁴⁹

PETER PITCHLYNN'S JOURNAL

In addition to the context of Choctaw history, another major consideration with regard to Peter Pitchlynn's document is his status in the Choctaw Nation, which bears on his motives for writing it. Peter Pitchlynn was definitely part of the new mixed-blood leadership that was rising in the Nation. He was the son of John Pitchlynn, an English trader who settled in the Choctaw Nation, married a Choctaw woman, and became an interpreter and a significant intermediary between the Choctaw leadership and agents of the United States government during the late eighteenth century. John's first wife died and he married Sophia Folsom, a daughter of Ebenezer Folsom, one of three brothers of Scotch-Irish descent who entered the Choctaw Nation in the late eighteenth century and married Choctaw women who were nieces of Mushulatubbee. Sophia was thus of mixed white and Choctaw descent, and in 1806 she bore her husband a son, Peter.[50] Peter became convinced of his need for formal education when he learned that a young Choctaw man had actually written a letter to James Madison, and even more convinced when he was befriended by Gideon Lincecum, a physician and naturalist and student of Choctaw history. Peter left home at the age of fourteen to go to a mission school somewhere in Tennessee (although its exact location is not clear from his papers). He enrolled in a Chickasaw school, Charity Hall, and he spent at least a year in an academy in Columbia, Tennessee. Although his education seems disjointed, he discovered interests in moral philosophy, poetry, history, biography, Choctaw mythology, medicine, and natural philosophy (the latter three subjects possibly through his contact with Lincecum). He served as a captain of the Choctaw lighthorsemen, the policing body established under the terms of the Treaty of Doak's Stand, thus demonstrating his desire for positions of leadership.[51]

David Baird questions the reasons for Peter's involvement in the 1826 council, given his father John's support of American policy.[52] Another consideration is the fact that this is a written document, which indicates the growing importance of literacy in the Nation. Marcia Haag and Henry Willis, the translators of the document in this book, comment in their preface that the widespread use of written Choctaw is surprising at this date, given that Cyrus Byington had just introduced his writing system in 1823 in the schools established by the American Board of Commissioners for Foreign Missions.

Pitchlynn had attended the school in Kentucky established by Richard Johnson and supported by Mushalutubbee's contribution of the

INTRODUCTION

Choctaw payment from the Treaty of 1825. Although Peter was related by marriage to the Folsom family, and his brother-in-law David Folsom was a strong supporter of the American Board missionaries and the schools they established, Peter did not attend any of those schools, which stressed the development of literacy in Choctaw and English. Indeed, his relative David Folsom worked closely with the American Board missionaries Cyrus Byington and Loring Williams in translating various books of the Bible into Choctaw and developing textbooks in Choctaw for the schools. It is unclear how Peter developed his own literacy in Choctaw, unless it was through his wife's influence, but the spelling system he used in this document was that developed by Cyrus Byington with David Folsom's assistance. Peter's and John's political connections with Mushalutubbee earned them the enmity of David Folsom, especially in the period of upheaval in 1825–26, and therefore it was unlikely that Peter would have learned directly from Byington, but Peter was well-educated and biliterate.

Although Baird particularly describes the formation of a constitution at a council on August 5, 1826, convened by Folsom and LeFlore as elected leaders of the Western and Northeastern Districts, at which Peter Pitchlynn served as a representative of the Northeastern District and as secretary of the meeting, the document translated here is not a constitution per se but a body of laws passed, as Pitchlynn explains, by "the Elected Council" in an effort to be of value to the nation (p. 45).

The details of the structure of the government described in Pitchlynn's journal are very sketchy, certainly more so than those included in the *Eighteenth Annual Report*. He notes that there will be three chiefs, "the main representatives, and the alternate," and the body will meet twice a year. Every district captain will have a "military assistant," which seems

31

to indicate that only adult males can hold this position, since men were involved in warfare, not women. "Those in charge" (presumably the district captains and their assistants) shall proceed to elect statesmen, but an election process is not spelled out, and the qualification for election is contained in the phrase a "person knowledgeable of the law," which is translated as "statesmen" (p. 47). But since the purpose of the 1826 gathering was to begin developing a code of laws, the implication seems to be that those present at the council or district leaders who had already set out their own codes of laws would be eligible for election. The captains' assistants were "authorized to counsel" and "sit with the speakers and be as a speaker."

The traditional precontact Choctaw social/political unit included the mingo, or chief, elder men respected for their wisdom, young men who had not yet killed in battle, and women and children. The mingo often had a man designated as his speaker (tishu miko) who spoke for him in councils. The captains' assistants mentioned in Pitchlynn's document may be a continuation of that status role as speaker for the chief.[53]

The journal states that legislation passed in the councils had to be passed by unanimous agreement of all three chiefs, or if they did not agree, by unanimous agreement of the speakers, captains, and their assistants if all were present. The document acknowledges that the districts had always had laws addressing all concerns, but if those proved "problematic" or were laid aside, then all new laws must be approved by "the Nation" through the procedure laid out in this document and must apply equally to all persons. Each district chief was to appoint an eight-man committee (which seems to contradict the elective scheme laid out earlier). These committees were to agree to dates for four meetings a year, "to legislate all issues" (p. 53).

INTRODUCTION

The Pitchlynn document is also very specific on one point that obviously referred to past situations. "It shall be passed that the district allotment cannot be used to pay for personal debts of the leader." In 1805 at the Treaty of Mount Dexter, the monetary payment for land ceded by the Choctaws to the United States went to pay trading debts accrued by Mushulatubbee and Apuckshanubbee.[54] The "nation's Elders" were also to attend these meetings and were to oversee the use of money allotments. "They will see to it that the wanton, unlawful use of these funds does not happen." These men thus constituted a kind of special finance committee for the new government, but again, the formation of this 1826 group seems to be prompted by the specific past actions of Mushulatubbee with regard to the annuity for education.

Although the intention of these laws was to bring about common action, the council members recognized that "some of the people seated here may create disturbances and hindrances" and declared that such people may be "detained." This action thus creates a new national category of crime—political dissent—which had previously been handled by discussion in each district, rather than imprisonment. Dissenters could now be arrested by "selected officers."

The first section of the Pitchlynn document is dated August 5, 1826, and Moses Foster and P. P. Pitchlynn are listed as scribes. It falls within the time frame for the council called by Folsom and LeFlore, but it differs significantly from the record of this meeting published in the American Board document. It also goes on to record laws of the people of the Northeastern District, referred to as the Potato Eaters, into 1828. Despite the council's stated mission to bring leaders of the three districts together in effectiveness and "a common mind," issues in the districts are still to be handled by committees directed by the chiefs. Since the chiefs were

33

now mixed-bloods—Greenwood LeFlore, David Folsom, and ultimately, in the Southern District, Samuel Garland—many provisions of the laws pertain to new economic situations, such as the disbursement of annuity money, collection of debts, and sale of tribal land.

The three districts continued to make their own law codes within the new framework. The new framework did, however, represent a change in the way things were being done in the Nation, a change that was acknowledged in Clause 21 of the Pitchlynn document (p. 50): "If the new Choctaw laws that are being legislated are quite problematic, and if the old laws are completely laid aside and forgotten, this new law needs to be permitted and approved by the Nation, through this procedure." The Choctaws now had a systematic way to establish a new body of laws.

Clauses 23–24 record the council's position on perhaps the most significant issue facing the Nation at that time—Choctaw land and its common ownership: "The land where we reside belongs to all who are called Choctaw people. If any single district wants to sell its land, and the other two districts do not agree, the single district cannot sell its land."

The protection of tribal resources was another issue. Article 30 reflects back to the Treaty of 1805, which settled personal debts of Mushulatubbee and Apukshanubbee with tribal land: "It shall be passed that the district allotment cannot be used to pay for personal debts of the leader." Clause 31 mitigated the previous article, however, by providing a mechanism to approve such payments. It may also indicate a remaining element of respect for the district leaders: "It shall be passed, however, if the standing eight-man committee of each of the other districts' standing committees decide to approve this, then it is approved." Clauses 33–39 also deal specifically with financial matters of the tribe, an obvious response to the new economic situation in which it found itself.

INTRODUCTION

Clause 40 is an important statement of tribal sovereignty, the ability of the Nation to determine its own membership: "And so it is, the white American citizens are not counted with us who are named Choctaws." For the Choctaw Nation in Indian Territory after the removal of 1830, the regulation of white Americans into the Nation and especially the marriages of whites and Choctaws was a major concern, but it is clear from this document that Choctaw leaders were concerned very early on with defining their own membership.

It was also clear in provision 41 that the Choctaw Nation was seeking to clarify its relationship with the United States government: "If any white citizen damages the properties of the Choctaws, these committees will, while in order, turn the entire matter over to the White authorities."

Clause 71 is a final declaration of nationhood: "It shall be thus. We are named the Choctaw people: a house shall be constructed at an established place." This establishment of a "house," a place of residence for the "Choctaw people" as a self-governing nation, stands in this document as an assertion of Choctaw nationhood in the face of relentless pressure from the United States government and the state of Mississippi for the Nation's removal to the lands west of the Mississippi River.

Pitchlynn's document, written in the Choctaw language by a man of mixed Choctaw-white heritage, in a time of political turmoil, offers new insights into the ways in which the Choctaw Nation's leaders were dealing with the extraordinary forces of political and cultural change at work during the 1800s. Although it is impossible to discern historically what was happening in the lives of Choctaw people who were still living on the land in their traditional villages in the Southeast, the decisions that were being made at the federal government level and by their own Choctaw leaders would ultimately affect them.

INTRODUCTION

This edition of Pitchlynn's journal, with its careful English translation and original Choctaw text, provides insight into the struggle of the Choctaw Nation to maintain its identity against the overwhelming forces of an advancing American nation. The contemporary Choctaw Nation in the twenty-first century remains a significant political force, and its treaty relationships from the 1800s with the United States government are still recognized.

After the Choctaws were finally moved to the western lands after the Treaty of Dancing Rabbit Creek in 1830, they restored their government by instituting subsequent constitutions beginning in 1834. These constitutions largely followed the models of those in surrounding states, mainly Arkansas. They regulated marriage, the treatment of slaves, and tribal governance. All of these subsequent constitutions represent the evolution of Choctaw government. This early document, recorded by Peter Pitchlynn beginning in 1826 and newly translated in this book, reveals insights from an original Choctaw perspective on how the Nation's leaders sought to uphold traditions of Choctaw leadership while responding to political, economic, and cultural changes that thrust the needs of the Choctaw Nation into direct conflict with the demands of the United States government.

INTRODUCTION

NOTES

1. Scholarship on Choctaw/European relations in the colonial era of American history in the early twentieth century has been largely in the form of unpublished doctoral dissertations. See, for example, Charles William Paape, "The Choctaw Revolt: A Chapter in the Intercolonial Rivalry in the Old Southwest," PhD diss., University of Illinois, 1946. More current scholarship in the late twentieth century has come with the growth of the academic field of American Indian Studies. See Greg O'Brien, *Choctaws in a Revolutionary Age, 1750–1830* (Lincoln and London: University of Nebraska Press, 2002) and James Taylor Carson, *Searching for the Bright Path: The Mississippi Choctaws from Prehistory to Removal* (Lincoln and London: University of Nebraska Press, 1999). Patricia Galloway has published a number of important articles on French-Choctaw relations, which culminated in her book *Choctaw Genesis, 1500–1700* (Lincoln and London: University of Nebraska Press, 1995). Tribal efforts to retain and revitalize tribal language have also made it possible to access documents such as the one in this book.

2. W. David Baird, *Peter Pitchlynn: Chief of the Choctaws* (Norman: University of Oklahoma Press, 1986), 27; Angie Debo, *The Rise and Fall of the Choctaw Republic* (Norman: University of Oklahoma Press, 1934), 48–49.

3. Lester Hargrett, *A Bibliography of the Constitution and Laws of the American Indians* (Cambridge: Harvard University Press, 1947), 554–55.

4. American Board of Commissioners for Foreign Missions, *Report of the American Board of Commissioners for Foreign Missions, Compiled from Documents Laid Before the Board, at the Eighteenth Annual Meeting, Which was Held in the City of New York, October 10, 11, 12, 13 & 15, 1827* (Boston: Printed for the Board by Crocker and Brewster, 1827), 122. Hereafter cited as *Eighteenth Annual Report*.

5. *Eighteenth Annual Report*, Appendix 4.

6. Ibid, 2–3.

7. Gideon Lincecum, "Choctaw Traditions about their Settlement in Mississippi and the Origin of their Mounds," *Publications of the Mississippi Historical Society* 8 (1904), 524–42; Jerry Bryan Lincecum and Edward Hake Phillips, eds., *Adventures of a Frontier Naturalist: The Life and Times of Dr. Gideon Lincecum* (College Station: Texas A&M University Press, 1994).

INTRODUCTION

8. John R. Swanton, *Source Material for the Social and Ceremonial Life of the Choctaw Indians*, Smithsonian Institution, Bureau of American Ethnology, Bulletin 103 (Washington, D.C.: Government Printing Office, 1931), 5–6, 36.

9. Galloway, *Choctaw Genesis*, 3.

10. Galloway, *Choctaw Genesis*, 282, 336, 359–60; Swanton, *Source Material*, 55, 57. American Board of Commissioners for Foreign Missions, Papers, Houghton Library, Harvard University, *Mayhew Journal*, August 8, 1822, ABCFM, vol. 1, folder 86; H. B. Cushman, *History of the Choctaw, Chickasaw, and Natchez Indians*, edited by Angie Debo (New York: Russell & Russell, 1962; reprint, introduction by Clara Sue Kidwell, Norman: University of Oklahoma Press, 1999), 88; Hoolamataha laws; *Mayhew Journal*, August 8, 1822, ABCFM, vol. 1, folder 86; *Missionary Herald* 29, no. 1 (January 1823): 6.

11. Galloway, *Choctaw Genesis*, 255–56.

12. Spratt defined the three districts geographically as the Northeastern District: "Beginning at old Fort Tombecbe, near the present town of Epes, Alabama, an old trail ran almost west to a ford on Sucarnatchie river near Narkesta, Mississippi, and then the trail passed on to Kushak bolukta tvmaha (Round reedbrake town) in what is now the southwestern corner of Kemper county, Mississippi"; the Southeastern District: "all south of it was in the Southeastern District. All the Districts cornered at this town of Kushak bolukta, or quite near it for the town itself lay within the Northeastern District"; and the Western District: "The Western District was rather long from north to south and was known as the Okla Falaia or "Long people" for that reason. North of Kushak belakta it bordered the Northeastern District and south of that town it bordered the Southeastern." See Richard Spratt, Notes on Choctaw Indians (University of Alabama, McClure Library), 49.

13. Cushman, *History of the Choctaw*, 27; Swanton, *Source Material*, 2, 77.

14. Swanton, *Source Material*, 174–79.

15. Cushman, *History of the Choctaw*, 27–28. Modern spellings and translations would be: Haiyip tuklo (Two Lakes), Hattak falaia (Long people), Okla hannali (Six Towns people), Apela (the Allies), and Chikasha (Chickasaws).

16. Swanton, *Source Material*, 2, 56; H. S. Halbert, "District Divisions of the

Choctaw Nation," in *Transactions of the Alabama Historical Society* 1: 375–85. The Pitchlynn journal spells Ahepat Okla as Ahepvtukla.

17. John Swanton, "An Early Account of the Choctaw Indians," in *Memoirs of the American Anthropological Association* 5 (1918): 22. The Choctaw spelling for chief is *miko* rather than *mingo,* and the Choctaw word for speaker is *tishu <u>miko</u>. Taskalusa* (black warrior) is clearly an error of Swanton's.

18. H. S. Halbert, "District Division of the Choctaw Nation," in *Publications of the Alabama Historical Society, Miscellaneous Collection* 1 (1901): 375, 377; Anna Lewis, *Chief Pushmataha, American Patriot: The Story of the Choctaws' Struggle for Survival* (New York: Exposition Press, 1959); Gideon Lincecum, *Pushmataha: A Choctaw Leader and His People* (Tuscaloosa: University of Alabama Press, 2004).

19. Cushman, *History of the Choctaw,* 243–60.

20. Cushman, *History of the Choctaw,* 273; Lincecum and Phillips, *Frontier Naturalist,* 74, 77–78.

21. Lincecum and Phillips, *Frontier Naturalist,* 76–77.

22. Cushman, *History of the Choctaw,* 274.

23. Lewis, *Chief Pushmataha,* 19.

24. Lewis, *Chief Pushmataha,* 16–17.

25. Cushman, *History of the Choctaw,* 235–38.

26. Charles J. Kappler, *Indian Affairs: Laws and Treaties.* 5 vols. (Washington, D.C.: Government Printing Office, 1904–41).

27. Kappler, *Indian Affairs,* vol. 2, 56–68, 63–64, 68–70, 87–88.

28. *Ibid.,* 137.

29. *Ibid.,* 191–93.

30. Jedidiah Morse, *A Report to the Secretary of War of the United States, on Indian Affairs. Comprising a Narrative of a Tour Performed in the Summer of 1820, under a Commission from the President of the United States, for the Purpose of Ascertaining, for the Use of the Government, the Actual State of the Indian Tribes in Our Country . . .* (New Haven, Conn.: Davis and Force, 1822). John F. Schermerhorn, "Report Respecting the Indians Inhabiting the Western Parts of the United

States," *Collections of the Massachusetts Historical Society*, 2d ser., 2 (1814); reprint, Boston: Charles C. Little and James Brown, 1846.

31. Kingsbury and Williams to Worcester, Yallobusha, June 29, 1818, ABCFM, vol. 1, folder 4; Loring S. Williams to Samuel Worcester, Yallobusha, June 20, 1818, ABCFM, vol. 2, folder 4.

32. 3 Stat. at Large 516. An Act Making Provision for the Civilization of the Indian Tribes Adjoining the Frontier Settlements. March 3, 1819.

33. ABCFM, vol. 1, folder, 63; John McKee to John C. Calhoun, Choctaw Agency, June 10, 1819, NA-LSW-R, roll 2, frame 1263; Kingsbury to Samuel Worcester, French Camps, August 9, 1819, ABCFM, vol. 2, folder 31; Kingsbury to Choctaw Chiefs, August 11, 1819, ABCFM, vol. 2, folder 33; Journal of Elliot Mission, August 9, 1819, ABCFM, vol. 1, folder 1, p. 8; Cyrus Kingsbury to Samuel King and Robert Bell, Elliot, December 18, 1819, ABCFM, vol. 2, folder 46.

34. Kappler, *Indian Affairs*, vol. 2, 191.

35. Cushman, *History of the Choctaw*, 328.

36. Cushman, *History of the Choctaw*, 70; Kappler, *Indian Affairs*, vol. 2, 213.

37. Cushman, *History of the Choctaw*, 331.

38. This important Choctaw leader's name is spelled many ways. His name appears in the August 5, 1826, entry spelled Nitakechi ('the commencement of the day'). Cyrus Byington also spells the name this way.

39. Cushman, *History of the Choctaw*, 342.

40. Carolyn Foreman, "The Choctaw Academy," *Chronicles of Oklahoma* 6 (December 1928): 453–80; 9 (December 1931); 382–411; 10 (March 1932): 77–114; J. L. McDonald to Tho. L. McKenney, Jackson, Mississippi, April 15, 1826, NA-OLA, Reel 169, Frame 160.

41. Lincecum and Phillips, *Frontier Naturalist*, 76.

42. Samuel Garland was elected under the new "Constitution" to be chief of the Southern District, but Nitakachi refused to acknowledge him. He later moved west and became a successful planter. See James C. Milligan, *The Choctaw of Oklahoma* (Abilene, Tex.: H. V. Chapman & Sons, 2003), 178.

INTRODUCTION

43. Thoburn, Joseph B., and Muriel H. Wright, *Oklahoma: A History of the State and Its People*, 2 vols. (New York: Lewis Historical Publishing Company, 1929) vol. 2, 788-89.

44. Cushman, *History of the Choctaw*, 283-84.

45. Kingsbury to Jeremiah Evarts, Mayhew, August 8, 1825, ABCFM, 18.3.4, Vol. 3.

46. Ray Holder, *The Mississippi Methodists 1799-1983: A Moral People "Born of Conviction"* (n.p.: Maverick Prints, 1984), 32-34.

47. 22nd Congress, 1st sess., H. Doc. 194, Board of Commissioners—Foreign Missions, *Memorial of the Prudential Committee of the American Board of Commissioners for Foreign Missions, Respecting the Property of the Board in the Choctaw Nation,* April 2, 1832, 1-5.

48. Baird, *Peter Pitchlynn*, 26; Arthur H. DeRosier, Jr., *The Removal of the Choctaw Indians* (Knoxville: University of Tennessee Press, 1970), 89; Thomas L. McKenney, *Memoirs: Official and Personal* (Lincoln: University of Nebraska Press, 1973), 244.

49. Thomas L. McKenney, *Reports and Proceedings of Col. McKenney, on the Subject of His Recent Tour Among the Southern Indians, as Submitted to Congress with the Message of the President.* Washington, D.C.: Printed by Gales and Seaton, 1826 [1827]); 19th Congress, 2d Session, Sen. No. 248, *Refusal of the Chickasaws and Choctaws to Cede Their Lands in Mississippi,* January 15, 1827, American State Papers, vol. 2, 708-18.

50. Baird, *Peter Pitchlynn*, xvii.

51. Baird, *Peter Pitchlynn*, 20-21; Charles Lanman, "Peter Pitchlynn, Chief of the Choctaws," *Atlantic Monthly* 26 (April 1870), 486-98.

52. Baird, *Peter Pitchlynn*, 27.

53. Swanton, *An Early Account*, 22.

54. Kappler, *Indian Affairs*, vol. 2, 69-70.

A Gathering of Statesmen

Photograph of the first page of Pitchlynn's bound journal containing the record of the 1826 council. It is stained and darkened, but readable with patience and knowledge of the language. Reprinted by permission from the Western History Collections, University of Oklahoma Libraries.

AUGUST 5, 1826

1 Chahta Hochitoka Moma Anumpuli itvnaha ^kvs[1] (a) nitak ont isht tahlapi; afvmmi mvt tahlepa sipokni achvfa; tahlepa untuchina pokoli tuklo akucha hanali aiena;

2 Yvmohmi hocha hatvk holitopa vhleha, tvshka chiputa, itvpehvt chiya kvt, ulhti tuchina Chahta okla pia ha hocha itahobvt vnumpulit e chiya hvt 3 nanta hona il apihisa kak ocha pim okla mvto achukmvt pin talaia hinla cho? il aiahnashke. 4 A numpa mak kia pim a

1 The elected Council met on the fifth day of August, in the year one thousand eight hundred twenty-six;

2 And so it is, elected people, the military, gathered in session, we are the three districts of the Choctaw nation, and gathered in session to conference:

3 What value can we provide for our nation? This shall be our concern.

4 These concerns are,

---

1. Pitchlynn often inserted respellings above the line, sometimes using a carat symbol, other times without it.

nukfila kvt il achvfa ke-
yu hosh okla pia kvt il a-
hashwa kvt ili pi ai vlhpie
so. hocha il ahashwa pullash
ke. **5** Pi yvmohmi pulla
hocha nana ka ik piachuk-
mo pulla il akostininchi
pin taiyaha. **6** Pi yvmohmi
hocha il ahashwakmvt
pim okla talaia anumpa
ilvppvt vlhpisvt taiyahak
ma ashuali hocha il a-
   [insert]²
hashwa makinlashke **7**   Il
aiahni hocha anumpa
vlhpisa ilvppv iklawo ka
il apihisvshke.
8 Anumpa aishtia vm
mona kvt ilvppak oke.

that those of us here continue to
not be of one mind, and we are
ineffective.

5 It is necessary for us to finally
conclude that we are certainly
not effective at the things we are
doing. **6** If we continue to work
and to finalize this legislation it
shall be worth the time and effort
for our nation.

7 And we shall proceed to pass a
few of these laws.

8 This is the first article.

---

2. Two or three undecipherable words—possibly in English—appear in the space between these lines. *Ashuali* in the line above is most likely *aiali*.

AUGUST 5, 1826

9 Hatak hochitoka anumpulit itvnaha kvt ont afvmmi achvfa a itintaklaka ai it vnaha kvt hitukla: 10 ilvppak ona nana puta moma apesa hocha itvnahashke 11 Yvmoh mi kvt hatak anumpuli chito ma aiahli achukma kvto, pehlichi tuchina hocha itvnaha hona itvnaha aiahli hona hochihifashke.

12 Yvmohmikmvt ulhti a ilaiyuka ya kvpitvni vhleha; yvmohmikmvt nakni tvshka achvfa hatak kvpitvni ma alapalashke 13 Yvmohmi kvt ishahli mvto, hatak nana apesa yona atokoli tok ona

9 Legislators shall meet twice within one year

10 and assemble to legislate all the agenda at this time.

11 And so it is, the best of our main legislators—three chiefs, the main representatives, and the alternate shall be on the roll.

12 It shall be thus: every district captain shall have a military assistant[3] assigned to him.

13 It shall be that those in charge shall proceed to elect statesmen.[4]

---

3. *Nakni tvshka* means 'male warrior'.

4. *Hatak nana apesa* is a 'person knowledgeable of the law'.

yvhmohmit aiashashke.

14 Nakni tvshka achvfa ilvppa nan vlhtoho̱ka kvt hatak itvnaha, hatak anumpuli ya ibataklat binili kvt anumpuli makinlashke **15** Ik yvmohmi kia hatak anumpuli hona iba takla ma binili keyu hokmvt nana anumpula hekeyushke yvmohmi kvt i̱ kvpitvni ho pulla iakaiya hoke—

16 Yvmohmikmvt anumpa nana vlhpisa kvt, kvpitvni, nana apesa, holitopa, moma kvt anumpa ma yvmma fehna kvt vlhpisashke: achit aiokpanchit intaiyahakma anumpa vlhpisa mvto aia̱ hli hocha hlipulli makinlashke.

14 This particular assistant is authorized to counsel. He shall sit with the speakers and be as a speaker.

15 If he does not sit with the speakers he shall not be allowed to speak; he shall be an alternate to the captain.

16 And so it is that these laws shall be mandated when all the captains, legislators, and elected persons are in complete and unanimous agreement:
having stated that, these laws have been approved and are completed.

AUGUST 5, 1826

2[5]

17 Hatak miko moma, iktuklo hokia vlhpiesa aiahnikmá. Yvmohmi kia hatak miko mvt ik aivlhpiesoshke, ~~aiahmikma~~ ahanchi kvt tuklo kia aiahnikma anumpa vlhpisa mvto ik aiahlo makinlashke 18 Yvmohmi kia hatak anumpuli vhleha, kvpitvni puta, in tvshka a chvfa i kvpitvni alapali ma chiya kvt kaniohmi kia anumpa mvto vlhpisa; makinlashke; 19 ahni mvto in taiyahakma, anumpa nana fehna hatuk mvt aiahlit ~~makinli~~ vlhpiesashke
20 Yvmohmikmvt ulhti ilaiyuka nanvlhpisa in

17 If all the leaders think something is valid even if it has not been seconded, or if the head man says it is not valid or two think it is not valid, this law shall not pass.

18 However, if the speakers, the captains, and the attachés of the captains are present, they may override the decision.

19 Whenever and however these decisions are finalized, these important words shall have been ratified.

20 So it is that each district has always possessed laws,

---

5. The numeral 2 was placed above the word *iktuklo,* meaning 'not two' or 'not seconded' based on the English 'second'.

    tuyula chatok, hatak tikba
    vhleha nana puta moma
    na imvlhpisa chatuk;
    nanavlhpisa intuyula;

21 yvmohmi kvt Chahta okla
    ilvppa anumpa himona
    vlhpihisa kvno et isht atalaklvm-
    mi chiyuhmikma kvn
    iakma itonlat ahaksit kvn
    iakma, anumpa himona
    ilvppa vlhpisa pulla hocha
    aiahlit pim okla talaia
    onah hlipulli makinlashke—

22 Yvmohmishke—Anumpa
    a ishtia ont atukla kvt ilvp
    pak oke.

23 Yakni ilvppa il aiahan-
    ta kvt Chahta okla e moma

    In the past, our forefathers always had laws for all concerns.

21 If the new Choctaw laws that are being legislated are quite problematic, and if the old laws are completely laid aside and forgotten, this new law needs to be permitted and approved by the Nation, through this procedure.

22 And so it shall be—This is the beginning of the second article[6] of the law.

23 The land where we reside belongs to all who are called Choctaw people.

---

6. *Anumpa* could be translated as either 'amendment' or 'article'. It refers to a section of the law.

pi hochih̲ifo kak̲o pimmi hoke.

24 Yvmohmi ka ulhti achvfa nanta hocha i̲ yakni atuka ulhti tuklo kvt vlhpiesa, aiahni keyu ka ulhti achvfa kvt ilap achvfvt yakni kancha hekeyushke

25 Yvmohmishke Anumpa aishtia ont atuchina kvt ilvppakoke.

26 Ilvppa yakohmashke.... Ulhti achvfa aiyuka ya hatak untuchina ho Committie, m̲iko vt atokolashke 27 Yvm ohmikma hatak ilvppa nan vlhtohoka kvto Chahta okla talaia ka nanishtim ai achukma he bieka hona aiahni hocha nanapesachi kvto

24 If any single district wants to sell its land, and the other two districts do not agree, the single district cannot sell its land.

25 It shall be thus. This is the beginning of the third article of the Law.

26 This shall be.... Each district shall have an eight-man committee, commissioned by the chief.

27 It is decreed that these men who have been selected shall determine laws to achieve the full well-being of the Choctaw nation, and these lawmakers shall be put into place.

hielashke 28 Yvmohmikmvt anumpa vlhpisa puyula vlhpih̲isa tuk vt aiahlit fullota he bieka mako—apesahanchashke— 29 Yvmma chiyuhmi: Im ulhti aiahanta bieka nana akvniohmi vlhpih̲isa chikma i̲ mi̲ko atukma aiyuka a-chvfa hocha im anumpa ma ieshi; hieli hocha nana puta moma mvno—i̲ mi̲ko atukma itimanumpvhonli pulla hocha nana puta mo ma kvno aia̲hlichi makin lashke.

30 Yvmohmi Hatak mi̲ko vto ilap bieka hocha nana kvno aheka ihi̲kbi tuk ma

28 And so, if all the laws have been agreed upon unanimously, they shall be valid.

29 It shall become law that when the officials of each district are in place, acting and passing laws, each must pledge loyalty to his leader[7] and communicate all of this information to the leader.

30 It shall be passed that the district alloment cannot be used to pay for personal debts of the leader.

---

7. The word *mi̲ko* is often translated as 'chief' but it can refer to leaders other than the primary chief of a band or tribe.

nanvlhpita yokvto isht vlhtolba hekeyushke. **31** Ikyvm ohmi kia Committee hatak untuchena hiele mvto im ulhti achvfa nana apesa hieli mvto, vlhpiesvshke; aiahni hokmvno; aiahli makinlashke.

31 It shall be passed, however, if the standing eight-man committee of each of the other districts' standing committees decide to approve this, then it is approved.

32 Yvmma chiyuhmi: ilvppa Committee vhleha nanvlhtoka tok ulhti tu china hieli kvto yakni ai‑iklvnna kanima hona, yvmmak ocha vlhpiesah, aiahnik mvto in taiyahak mvt afvmmi achvfa a‑itintaklakvno ushtaha ita famvt chiyvt im okla talaia nana akaniohmi puta

32 Whereas, these committees that were commissioned by the three districts,[8] shall agree to set dates for four meetings within a year, somewhere convenient within the interior of the nation, to legislate all issues.

---

8. This refers to the standing eight-man committees.

kvno apesa makinlashke

33 Yvmohmi. Yakohmit chi yakmvt im okla talaia ho chitoka vhleha Committee anumpulit itahoba hoke, achashke.

34 Yvmohmi kvt nanvlh pita tvli holisso vt Chahta okla talaia nanisht ayuk pahe bieka hona isht vlhpih̲isashke 35 Nanisht yopula ka yvmma imma ka isht ikvlhpieso ka kia pi h̲isashke Committee ilvppa hieli kvt nana puta moma ka achukmalit nana ka akostininchashke—

36 Nanaheka puta nanakia Chahta okla hatukma aiishtlokowak

33 And so. It has been declared that the nations' elders[9] shall gather there to conference.

34 With respect to money allotments they will oversee their lawful use to benefit the Choctaw nation.

35 They will see to it that the wanton, unlawful use of these funds does not happen. This standing Committee shall carefully research and be aware of all matters.

36 When all and whatever bills are presented to the Choctaw nation for collection, this shall be the procedure.

---

9. *Hochitoka vhleha* refers to persons of status, who might generally be elders.

AUGUST 5, 1826

ma, yakohmishke, **37** aionat in taiyahakmvt hatak hochi toka itahoba aiashakvno, nanaheka mvto ika vlht piesokma ishit chukohowo makinlashke Nanaheka takali kvto aivlhpiesa keyukma ik aiokpahancho makinlashke— **38** Nanaheka mvto vlhpiesa makinli nanakia puta atvpa feh na pih̲isokma Committee ilvppa hieli kvt atvpa feh nvshke. **39** Achikmvto kvn vblit i̲ kanchikmvt aivlh piesa bieka ho—im aiokpahanchi makinlashke.
40 Yvmohmikma nahullo America vlheha piba

37 When the group of elders meets in session, if bills brought before them are inflated, they shall not be in order. If the bills are unlawful, they shall not be approved.

38 Even if the bills are correct, the Committee may see that the bills are excessive, and they should say it is too much.

39 If the committee declares it much too high, they can block it, and correct each bill and then declare it in order, so it can be passed.

40 And so it is, the white American citizens are not counted with us who are named Choctaws.

holhtiena keyu   41   hocha Chahta pia ha nana ka pim okpaha mikma Committee vlheha ilvppa pulla kvto nana akaniohmi puta ona a-chukmali momvt Nahullo miko atukma   42   itimikvno nana imokpunlo tukmvt im vlhtoba hetuk mak heto yvmohmvi makinlashke

43 Yvmohmi Hochitoka moma Chahtaokla hochito itahoba aiyuka ya Committee vto chitokaka moma Chahta hochifo itahoba chash itin tabla ya nana kanimi puta kvt yakohmi tok oke achit anvhonlashke.   44   Yvmohmik ma anumpa ilvppak ocha

41 If any white citizen damages the properties of the Choctaws, these committees will, while in order, turn the entire matter over to the White authorities.

42 It is not possible that the owner should not be compensated for the damages; this is how it shall be.

43 And it shall be proclaimed that all the representatives, each of the Choctaw officials assembled together, the Committee, higher officials, anyone who has not been restricted, state that this has been in practice.

44 And so it shall be stated that this whole law is beneficial to our people, is all proper, and that this is indeed our will.

AUGUST 5, 1826

hatak nanisht ayukpa hi ona vlhpisah bano—il aiahni tuk oke achit anvhonlashke.

× 45 Yvmohmashke Anumpa pes ~~svt~~ aishtia ont ^a^ ushta kvt ilvppak oke ×

45 This is the beginning of the fourth article of the Law.

46 Yakohmashke. Himaka nitak pilla ma hatak itahoba nana apesa aiasha kvt achukmvt nuktvlvt chiyvt nana pihisa kia hatak miko
7
ilvppa pulla kvt hatak ma achukmalit atokohonlashke[10]

46 It shall be thus. Henceforth, the chief shall carefully select these men, seated here, who are good, sensible, and alert, to be legislators.

47 Yvmohmikma nanvlh toka okla ilvppa hikia kvt nana akvniohmi puta mo ma, hochitoka vlheha, nanapesa yvmohmik— mvt nanvlhpita kia hat

47 And so, the group of installed elected people, with all of their duties assigned, the arbiters, the officials, as well as a paymaster, have been seated.

---

10. Pitchlynn has various strikeouts, Xs, and insertions on this page. It is unclear what the inserted numeral 7 refers to.

ak chiya. **48** Ilvppa chiya kvno hatak kaniohmi kvt nana ka itaklvmmi kia ok pvni hocha aiahantakma im oktvbla he oke—
49 Yvmma chiyuhmikma kvna hocha hatak holitopa anumpuli aiasha kvno ik iyimmot anumpa im okpvnit ahanta kvt nana okpoyulo nana kia holitopa vhleha anum pohonli kvno isht apisa la he ma mihi yakmvno hatak nanvlhtoka tok yvmma hieli kvto ha lvllit yukachit ishi makinlashke **50** Yvmoh

48 However, some of the people seated here may create disturbances and hindrances. When they break the rules, and continue to do so, they shall indeed be detained.[11]

49 For example, if someone disagrees with the decrees of the elected officials, and in his disagreement continues to break the law, if I[12] should be the judge, whatever laws are broken shall be so judged by this present law, and he shall be detained and arrested by the selected officers.

50 When these elected officials pass judgment on him, he shall thus be charged.

---

11. *Im oktvbla* means to be stopped or kept from doing something.

12. Pitchlynn uses the first person "as an example" of how the judge might decide such a case.

ma hatak anumpuli ilvppa chiya kvt anumpa nana h<u>o</u> achit im vlhtahat <u>o</u> bohlikma aiahli makinlashke.

51 Yvmohmi hoke Anumpa aishtia ont isht tahla pi kvt ilvpp ak oke

51 It is indeed so. This is the beginning of the fifth article.

52 Committee vlheha vlhtoh<u>o</u>ka kvt kvpvssa tuklo ilvppa k<u>a</u> nanisht ahanta kvt vlhtokashke

52 The committees that were installed these past two winters shall be authorized to conduct business.

53 Yvmohmi cha Committie vlheha Chahta hochifo okla moyumvt itahobvt chiyakmvt hatak anumpuli <u>i</u> miko achvfvt ikbashke.

53 And so when the Committees, all those called Choctaw, are seated together, one shall be appointed leader.

54 NB Yvmma Committee chiya ka ahnit achvfvt peh lichi ka ikbashke[13]

54 NB The seated Committee will install one leader of their choosing.

---

13. Pitchlynn uses the notation NB, *nota bene* (take careful note), to add his own footnote here.

55 Yvmohmishke Anumpa aishtia ont isht hanali kvt ilvppakoke.

56 Yakohmashke hatak holitopa ~~nanvlhfv~~ nanvlhtoka puta in taiyaha hvt tok, anumpa puta anum pahonla hi ocha vlhtvho̱ka tukvt ilvppak ocha nana kvt vlhpisa hinla: aiah nikmvt anumpohon lash ke; vlhpiesakma, vlhpiesa aiahnikmat vlhpiesa; ahanchashke.   57 Amba ik vlh pieso aiahnikmvt ik vlh pieso aiahanchaskhke.

58 Yvmohmkishke. Anumpa a ishtia ont ishtuntuklo kvt ilvppakoke.

55 It shall be so. This begins the sixth article.

56 It shall be that the selected people shall have the right to speak. If the elected think that something is right, it should be justified. If he thinks it is right, it should be justified.

57 But if he thinks it is not right, he should say that it is not right.

58 It shall be so. This is the beginning of the seventh article.

AUGUST 5, 1826

59 Anumpa vlhpisa moma atia kia anuhumpa ka kvm vssat Chahta okla ha anumpa ilvppat intuyulashke   60 Hatak itvnaha chinto il achukma hocha nana il apihisashke

61 Yakokmvt nana apihisa akin li hosh—nitak inla nana kia anumpa hochash ik a‑chukmo chiyuhmishke.

62 Anumpa achvfa chohmi kia yvmohmi kvt takanli hokma shifit e kocha he akin lashke   63 Amba hatak anum puli pia hvt anumpa vlh pisa mvto achukma biekash ke, il ahiahnikmvt anum pa ilvppa achvfa kia e shifit

59 In the past we have always had laws; however the Choctaw people shall possess this series of strong laws.

60 We have efficient and great councilmen and we shall continue to legislate.

61 And so it is, we are thus passing laws—however, on other days, the same legislators may find the passed legislation does not meet standards.

62 If there is a mistake on the record, we shall erase it.[14]

63 But if we think the wording is correct, we the speakers shall not erase even one word.

---

14. The implication is that the mistake will be corrected.

e kancha he keyushke

64 Yvmma chiyvhmishke
Himaka nitak pilla ma
anumpa ilvppa il apihi̱sa
achukmalit chi chu̱kash
atukma foyuki achukmvt hvt
il itvnohowashke 65 Ik pim
mi hakso pullashke; 66 ahni
pin taiyaha hocha himaka
nitak fehna Akvs ~~12~~ 1826
(Akvs nitak ont isht tahlapi
micha AD 1826)— 67 hatak holi
topa vhleha tvshka puta
chiya hvt ulhti tuchina
Chahta okla pia hash ocha
itahobvt anumpulit e
cheya kvt pe hohchifo ha
anumpa ilvppa il apala
hinchishke

64 That is so. Now, in coming days we should take well to heart these laws we have passed as we continue our lives.

65 It is imperative that we not forget.

66 We conclude on this very day August ~~12~~ 1826 (August fifth, AD 1826)

67 The elected men, all the seated warriors, we the three Choctaw districts gathered and present to deliberate, our names shall be added to this document.

AUGUST 5, 1826

Tvpenahumma
David Folsom   } his ×mark[15] Miko   his mark
Greenwood Leflore   Chiefs

Yukohlo Hopaii ×
Washashimastvbi ×
Pistembi ×
Hopaii Iskitini ×
Hopaii humma ×   Hopaii, Kvpvtvni,   Shamans,[16] Captains, Warriors
Nitak echi ×   Tvshka.   (written vertically across the
Ofi humma ×   margin)
Tishu Miko ×
Iacha Hopaii ×
Samuel Cobb ×
Holvbi ×
Tvshka holehta ×
Lewis Perry ×
Ia hoka tvbi ×
Atuklvbi Tvshka ×

---

15. Most of the participants have × appearing after their names, and those names are all signed in the same hand as the text. Some do not include an × and we speculate that those men were literate.

16. *Hopaii* refers to persons who deal with the spiritual life: shamans, priests, but not those who practice medicine.

This photograph of pages 18–19 of the journal shows the beginning of the long list of signers from the first council meeting of August 5, 1826. Reprinted by permission from the Western History Collections, University of Oklahoma Libraries.

AUGUST 5, 1826

John Washington ×
Robert Folsom ×
Hoshishimataha ×
James Shields ×
Mishamaia ×
Koi humma ×
Ishtimilhishi ×
Tishu ×
Kvsh onahikat ×
Lauwintvbi ×
Ofi nowa × × ×
Miko hoyopa ×
Chahta im ataha ×
Ishtanukahacho ×
Hiopancha hvbi ×
James Pickens ×
Isaac James ×
Kvpitvni Ohlehko ×
Chilahi humma ×

Oklinla ×
John Garland ×
Weshakihi humma ×
Nvhlitvbi ×
Iapalvbi ×
William Hays ×
Atonochvbi ×
Itinahalvbi ×
Wakachvbi ×
Shapanvhahvbi ×
Kvniohikvbi ×
Lewis Durant ×
Hvshi humma ×
Pashi ishtikvbi ×
Achintvbi ×
Pahlinihvbi ×
Aiushkemo ×
Koi humma ×
James Comes ×

Shukha humma ×
Pisatvbi ×
Kisha humma ×
Kvsh ona holahta ×
Joseph Kincaid ×
Benjamin James ×
Tuli humma ×
Afamatvbi ×
Jeremiah Folsom ×
Tvshka holehta ×
William Wade ×
Tvnvpocha ×
Tahoka ×
Nitak vbi ×
Isifoni ×
Willis ×
Jesse Brashears
William Hall
Joel H Nail

William Foster

J L McDonald

Vaughan Brashears

68 Anumpa ilvppa vlh pihi̱sa kvt im anukfila achvfa bieka hocha chiyvt apesvt im vlhtaiyahvshk Moses Foster} Ilvppa ~~abi~~

~~vm~~

he
P P Pitchlynn ^moma ho e holissochi

68 The council, in session, has finalized this law and is in unanimous agreement.

We (Moses Foster and P. P. Pitchlynn) have documented all of this.

---

69 Hatak holitopa vhleha ita hobvt nanalhpesat chiya kvt Akvs 5th 1826 yvmohmi kvt anumpa ma apesat itim achvfvt pullvt in taiyahakvt anumpa aisht ia vmmona;   70 yvmmak

69 The legislators are assembled here in session August 5, 1826. And so it is necessary for the body to be in unison.

This is the first article.

70 We shall make our decisions, which have been made with reference to our previous decisions.

atuk ona aisht pimanukfi
lit nana pim anukfihin
lvshke

71 Yakohmashke. Chahta ok
la pe hochiefo; aboha hanta
vt yvmma fehna hona a
hiki ashke; il aiahnikma,
aboha hanta mvto tobvt pi
hikia akinlashke.   72 Ilvppa
yvmohmahe nanishtvlh
pisa kvt tvli holisso tahlepa
ushta pokoli tahlapit aiena
kvt nanvlhpita tvli holisso
chatuka ishtakochit mihi

    na
ocha nishtvlhtoba[17] hona aboha
hanta mvto pi hikiashke.

       his
Tvpena humma ×
       mark

David Folsom   } Aiokpvnit
Greenwood Leflore[18] } aiahlikvt

71 It shall be thus. We are named the Choctaw people; a house[19] can be constructed at an established place; if we wish to have that council house, it shall be constructed there for us.

72 This can be authorized with the withdrawal of four hundred and fifty dollars; this means it shall be payment for that council house that we shall have.

Approved and ratified

---

17. This is intended to be written *nanishtvlhtoba*.

18. Words and names are variously spelled throughout the journal: Tvpena humma (Tvpenahumma), Leflore (LeFlore).

19. *Aboha hanta* 'white house' refers to the color white as a symbol of peace, in contrast to red, hence a peace house. It is used to mean a council house.

6[20]

okla ahepvtukla nana imvlhpisa.

the law of the Ahepvtukla people.

Chahta Yakni Ahepvtukla
Chun 12th 1827

Choctaw Ahepvtukla Country
June 12th, 1827

73 Himak nitak fehna Kam mitti pia e chiya kvt ilvppa fehna hona pim anukfihinlashke.   74 Nanvlhpita tvli holisso pi maya chatuk vt tvli holisso tahlepa auatahlapi hocha a kvshapvt nanishtvlhpisa mak inlashke.   75 Yvmohmi kvt tvli aboa hiohli tuchina hosh isht vlhpisa makinlashke.

73 On this day, we, the Committee, in session, shall make our decisions on these issues.

74 The usual, on-going allotment that we have is fifteen hundred dollars, and it shall be divided by this rule.

75 And so the money shall be allocated for three smithies.[21]

76 Yvmohmikvt ahika achvfa ka tvli holisso tahlepa tahlapi hocha isht vlhpisashke il aiahnishke.

76 Our will is that each shall be budgeted at five hundred dollars.

---

20. Some of the pages have numerals, which may have been an internal reference system.

21. *Tvli aboa hiohli* is 'a place for working metal', such as a metalworks or blacksmith's.

JUNE 12, 1827

77 Ilvppa yakohmashke. Tvli aboa achvfa kvt Mecha (Major) Iahokatvbi, in chuka fehna ha̱ ahikiashke

78 Yvmohmik ma ontatuklo tvli aboa hikia kvt ~~Ma~~ Mecha (Major) Holvbi in chuka fehna hona ^a hiki ashke— 79 Yvmohmikma anowa Miko Lewi Folsom in chuka fehna he hikiash ke.

80 Yvmohmikma anowa tvli boli nana ithvna chi̱kvt tvli aboa hiohli ka ilvppa hatak vpi humma himita hocha ibafohkvt toksvlit tvli aboaka ithana makin lashke 81 Chekosi tvli boli

77 This shall be. One smithy shall be built on the home site of Major Iahokatvbi.

78 And then, a second smithy shall be built on the home site of Major Holvbi.

79 And then Chief Levi Folsom shall have a mall[22] constructed at his home site.

80 And so then smithing malls shall be constructed for the teaching of metalworking, which young Indian men shall be apprenticed to learn.

81 Soon they must be ready to be skilled smiths.

---

22. *Anowa* means 'mall' in the sense of 'grounds' or an open space that can be walked on.

impona, vlhtoka kia vlh-
taha pullashke— **82** Yvmoh
mikma ilvppa hatak vpi
humma \ tvli boli nana it
hvnach̲ikvt ilapinli hocha
il
nana i̶l̶ apelakma impa
puta: yohmi kia nanvlhto
ba kvt iekshokashke.

83 Yvmohmik mvt anowa
ilvppa yakohma he il aiahnishke. **84** Tvli aboa mvto nana
ha vlhtaha achukma cha
hikiak ma; **85** ponola ashana
isht ikba he puta; tvli ya ikbi
makinlashke— **86** Yvmohmik
mvt nanishtaiiska ilayuka
ya moma ma ikbahekeyu
ma **87** ulhti il achvfa nan

82 So then the Indian people will teach themselves metalworking, and they will have to provide their own board, because funds have never been provided for this.

83 Thus, we wish for this mall to be prepared in this manner.

84 These smithies shall be well-equipped;

85 and there shall also be manufactured all types of products of cotton fiber;[23] they shall be manufactured the same as metal— **86** And so it shall be enacted that with respect to all different tools that cannot be produced,

87 the council, in agreement, will withdraw and place in their hands money from the grant to buy augers[24] and spindles and also a place to manufacture these tools, like the other two—

---

23. *Ponola ashana* refers to all types of twisted spun cotton fiber, including rope, yarn, and cord.

24. *Nana ashana* refers to tools such as bolts, screws, augers, and threaders that penetrate a material.

JUNE 12, 1827

vlhpita pin tvli holisso a
aishtkochit nana ashana
isht ikbi a ishit chumpvt
nana ashana ikbi hiohli
tuklo chohmika ibbak ma
        a
fohki makinlashke—

88 Hatak anumpuli momvt vlhpiesa; aiahnit in tai yaha na anumpa ilvppvt aiahlit vlhpihisvshke.

88 All being proper speakers; we have scrutinized and enacted this law.

89 Kammitte vhleha pia kvt pi hohchifo kvt anumpa ilvppa e lapalihin chishke.

    Iahokalvbi ×
    Holvbi ×
    Pistembi ×   Kammitte
    Israel Folsom ~~Comm~~
    Miashembi ×

89 We the committee who are named here, we so attach our names to this law.

    Committee

Nvhlitvbi ×
Robert Folsom
Jeremiah Folsom × —
Lewi Folsom {Ahepvtukla
    i̲ Miko vt aiok
pvchit aiahlishishke

Chahta Yakni Ahepvtukla
Chun 12 1827

90 Himak nitak fehna ka Kommitte pia: hatak holi topa vhleha! itibvlhot e chiya kvt anumpa ilvppa il apih̲isvshke. **91** Himak a nitak pilla ma kvna hocha isuba ho h̲ukopa na anumpa mvto atokowvt taiyahlikma ititvpa kvto

Levi Folsom Chief of the Ahepvtukla approves

Choctaw Ahepvtukla Country
June 12, 1827

90 On this very day we the Committee: the authorized persons, we are assembled and seated to be enacting laws.

91 From this day forward, if someone steals a horse, and this accusation is proven, a switch[25] shall be put into the hands of the lighthorsemen for punishment.

---

25. *Iti tvpa* is a general term that could refer to a board, a switch, a cane, a stick, a pole, or other cut branch.

JUNE 12, 1827

isuba<u>o</u>menili tushka no-
ibbak ma foyukashke.

92 Yvmohmikma fahama tahlepa achvfa, ilefoka kia iksho nvli ma onochi mak inlashke—

93 Yvmohmikmat wak okma fahama pokoli tahlapi ilifoka kia iksho nvli ma onochi makinlashke—

94 Yvmohmikmvt shuk ha okma fahama pokoli tuchina kvt onatohonlashke.

95 Yomohmikmvt nana boshulli puta nana kia h<u>o</u>kopa kvt ahantahé. 96 Yvm ohmikma iti tvpa onvt ohonla kvt hatak nanapesa

92 And so then on this charge he will receive one hundred lashes, stripped of clothes, on his bare back—

93 And if it is a cow, he shall get fifty lashes, stripped of clothes, on his bare back for that charge—

94 And so it if it a pig, he shall receive thirty lashes.

95 And so, should someone steal small items,

96 the switch shall be used on him, but the judge may use his discretion to make lesser charges.

mvt ilvppak osh vlhpiesa;
aiahnit iklawo nana kia
onohonchashke.

97 Yvmohma he il api
hisvshke Kvna hocha
ahanta pulla tok ona
isuba ominili tvshka nan
apesa vhleha iti ishit yvm
ohmit mayakma hatak
haksi kash ocha nahalupa
ma ishi; yvmohmi kvt
tanampo; iskifa bvshpo
puta; nahalupa puta
momaka ishi oka hikiak
mvt nana okpvna hima
akot—yvmohmikma—
nana apiesa ilvppa okla
aya kvt fiopa ma intvbla
hi tuk ocha in tvblikma

97 We shall be enacting thus:
If an authorized lawman is
present while some man in a
drunk[26] condition is carrying a
sharpened weapon, a gun, all axes
and knives, all potential weapons;
if he was standing there, definitely
with one of these, breaking the
law when he does so, the lawman
may kill him, and if he does, he is
covered in his action.

---

26. *Haksi* is an important word that refers to any condition of being out of control, including drunk, duped, or bewitched, and is extended to be a general term of derogation.

JUNE 12, 1827

ituyula makinlashke **98** Yvm ohmikma anumpa hanta ma halvlli hocha yvmohmi ka okla nanapesa ilvppvt anumpa nanakia a isht in chukushpa hekeyu mak ona, **99** anumpuli kvt aia- hlit pim aiachvfvt taiya hishke

100 Anowa anumpa ilvppa il apih̲isashke. Kvna fehna hocha himaka pilla ma ok lu ak a ahepvtukla anum pa vlhpisa takali ka shitilema ishvla hi oke
hot ^ yvmohmi cha anumpa okpulo kia anumpohonli; isuba o̲ minili tvshka nana vlhpisa
~~apesa~~ ieshi ka nana kia

98 And so, in upholding the infallible law,[27] these legislators cannot take any statement and misrepresent it.

99 This law shall be ratified unanimously.

100 We shall mandate this law. From this day forward, if someone holds in contempt the existing laws of the Ahepvtukla and verbally abuses and threatens a lighthorseman, whatever he does,

---

27. *Anumpa ahanta* has the sense of a supreme law that supersedes others.

kvnimicha he ik mihi-
ha nana kia,   **101** isuba omi
nili tvshka mvto anum
pa kvllo achukma kvno—
ai itula mvto in taiyakash
ke.   **102** Ik kaniohmi nana
kia himak nitak pilla
mvno—nahalupa nanakia
tikba wieli hocha anum
pa hanta hashona aiahli
ha he nana hatuk mvt
ik yvmichi, nana kia vlh-
piesa makinlashke.   **103** Aiahnit
anumpuli mvt pintaiya
kashke.

104 Kommiti vhleha pia kvt
pi hochifo kvt anumpa ilvp
pa e lapalihinchishke

101 the lighthorsemen are authorized to carry out the law.

102 Let these things be from this day forward—if someone threatens with a sharp weapon, of any kind, if this be true, he shall be judged even if it was not used.

103 Our wishes shall be fulfilled.

104 We are the committee named here, and we attach our names.

JUNE 12, 1828

Iahokatvbi ×
Holvbi ×
Pistembi ×
Israel Folsom Kamiti   Committee
Miashambi ×
Nvhlitvbi ×
Robert Folsom
Jeremiah Folsom ×

 Lewi Folsom Ahepvtukla Levi Folsom Chief of the
  i Miko aiokpv   Ahepvtukla approves
  chit aiahlishke

 Yakni
Chahta ^Ahepvtukla[28] Choctaw Ahepvtukla Country
 Chun 12th 1828   June 12th, 1828

105 Yakohmakshke Himakmak ni **105** It shall be on this very day
tak ~~pulla ma~~ fehna ka

---

28. Beginning with this entry, Pitchlynn will insert the word *Yakni* 'land' above his place headings in nearly every entry, as if in correction of an error in having omitted it.

anumpa il apihisa kvt **106** himaka pilla ma Chahta ohoyo ho kanima hocha im vlla akinli ka chelit a hambikmvt iti tvpa kolofa ishit fahama pokoli tuchina akocha tahlapi, ili foka kia iksho, nipi bieka hona on vtohonlashke.

107 Yvmohmikma ihatak, keyukmvt ohoyo ha ai it ikhana peh kanima nana hocha vlla illa chi ka ai itvpela pullvt vlla tukma ahambi tukma aitvpela hatvk okvt fahama pokoli

106 the laws we are passing, from this day forward, if a Choctaw woman kills her child at birth, she will be charged with thirty-five lashes on her bare back with a switch.

107 And if her husband or someone she has known, whoever, helps her kill the child that is to die, the conspirators[29] shall receive thirty-five lashes on the bare back, without clothes.

---

29. *Itapela* means 'partner, those who help each other', in this case with a negative connotation.

JUNE 12, 1828

tuchina akocha tahlapi mak<u>o</u> ilifoka kia iksho nvli bieka ho onvtohonla mak inlashke.

108 Kamiti vhleha pia kvt pi hochifo kvt anumpa ilvp po e lapalihinchvshke.
    Iahokatvbi ×
    Holvbi ×
    Pistembi ×
    Israel Folsom
    Miashambi ×
    Nvhlitvbi ×
    Robert Folsom
    Jeremiah Folsom ×
	108 We are the Committee and we attach our names.

Lewi Folsom Ahepvtukla i̱ miko vt aiokpvchat aiahlichishke

Levi Folsom Chief of the Ahepvtukla approves

Chahta Ahepvtukla
Chun 12th 1828

Choctaw Ahepvtukla
June 12th 1828

109 Yakohmashke—Himak ^ ni-tak fehna anumpa ma ilvppa il apihi̱svshke.

109 It shall be—On this very day we shall be passing this statute.

110 Yvmohmi kvt ohoyo nana ahni keyu, peh a-chukma nana hokia nakni kanima hocha hok-lit ilbvshalechit okpahani tuk o̱; 111 anumpa mvto ato kowat mvt taiyahak ma, iti tvpa mvto fahama pokoli tuchina akocha tahlapi on

110 If a woman is unwilling, and a man violates[30] her by raping her

111 the law specifies that he shall be charged with thirty-five lashes with a switch.

---

30. *Ilbvshalechit okpahani* refers to causing harm, oppression, shame, or any form of distress, especially emotional.

JUNE 12, 1828

vtohonla makinlashke.

112 Kamiti vhleha pia hvt pi hochifo kvt anumpa ilvppa elapalihinchishke.

    Iahokatvbi ×
    Holvbi ×
    Pistembi ×
    Israel Folsom
    Miashambi ×
    Nvhlitvbi ×
    Robert Folsom
    Jeremiah Folsom ×
    Lewi Folsom Ahepvtukla
        i Miko vt aiokpvchit
        aiahlichishke

112 We are the Committee and we shall thus attach our names.

Levi Folsom Chief of the Ahepvtukla approves

Yakni	
Chahta Ahepvtukla	Choctaw Ahepvtukla Country
Akvs 26, 1828	August 26, 1828

a

113 Himak nitak fehna ka e-ahepvtukla kvpvtvni vhleha; holitopa vhleha makosh Chahta okla pia kvt e chiyvt nana il apihi svshke   114 Anumpa ilvppa fiena ka vlhpiesvshke; il aiahni kvt himaka nitak pilla ma.   115 Hatak a it i nukkilli; ai it ik im a-chuyukmo, nana kvt takan li chatukma, yakni chuko kashofvt wvt aiakshot ^ kvnia mak inlashke—

113 On this very day we the Ahepvtukla captains, the authorized people, we the Choctaw people are seated here to mandate all things.

114 This particular law shall be quite correct; we wish it to go from this day forward.

115 Men who hate each other, who disagree with each other, whatever other things have been going on, where it can be done, those disagreements shall be pardoned and forgiven.

August 26, 1828

116 Yvmma chiyuhmi, hatak vpi humma nana hokia illa hia im aiahni ho aya cha tuk nana kia himak nitak fehna kvno—ulhti achvfvt pia kvt akvshofvt kvniashke. 117 Yvm ohmi kvt hatak hikia puyuta, okla ahepvtukla hochihifo hocha hikiak mvt—anumpa vlhpisa ilvppa fehna kvt ai i hulla hi bieka hona hikiashke. Il aiahnishke.

118 Anumpa ma il aia hlichit pin taiyaha hocha anumpa hatuk mvno pukoli chvfa ha e lapalihinchishke

116 That being so, even if the Indian people wish that someone should die, from this very day, we of that particular district completely pardon him.[31]

117 And therefore, all the men present calling themselves the Ahepvtukla people, shall honor this very law. This shall be our will.

118 We the ten[32] have so concluded and attach our signatures to this law.

---

31. The judgment of the district that has jurisdiction shall prevail.

32. The ten appear to refer to the signatories apart from the chief and the hopaii.

Iahokatvbi ×
Holvbi ×
Miashambi ×
Hakluntvbi ×
Koi humma ×   Kamiti   Committee
Hishishi humma ×
Jeremiah Folsom ×
PP Pitchlynn
Benjamin James
Robert Folsom ×
Lewi Folsom Ahepitukla i   Levi Folsom Chief of the
   Miko vt aiok-   Ahepvtukla approves
   pvchit aioklichishke
Im oklvsha Hopaii   Tribal Shamans
Pitema Hopaii   Hopaii   Shamans
Hopaii Iskitini

August 26, 1828

| Chahta Ahepvtukla | Choctaw Ahepvtukla |
| Akvs 26, 1828 | August 26, 1828 |

119 Nana pim anukfihin lvshke. 120 Yvmohmi kvt nana ka yvmohma he ke yu nana kia hatak ho chukma, nana ma okpaiyanilashke: aiahni nana hosh yvmichi tok keyu kia nan vlhtoba mi hiona nana ka yvmohmio ke 121 Yvmohmikmvt vbi bvnna keyu; pilla im isht kvnvpvt illi; ik yvmohmi kia vlhtohomba he 122 Yvmohmi chatuk

119 We shall decide some matters.

120 There are men who are good, but who may do harm anyway. Even if someone did not intend to do harm, he will indeed give some compensation.

121 And so if someone did not intend to kill, but someone accidentally dies, let him be fined anyway.

122 It used to be this way,

nana kia himaka nitak
fehna kvna—anumpa
kvmvssa fehna kvno il api
hisvshke

123 Yvmma chiyuhmi
Himaka nitak pilla ma
yakohmashke.   124 Kvna hocha
hatak miko kano abi cha
iti vlli ma ik bahano; yvm
ohmi cha maleli hocha
kvniakma; itibapishi hoke;
in tek oke, in chuka achvfa,
i kanohmi puyuta; aiasha
kvto nana hona okpaha
ni tok keyu kvto nana
ma a ishtilbvshvt hoto-
hompa he keyushke.

but from this day forward, we will decide stricter laws.

123 It shall be thus from this day forward.

124 If someone kills the chief without reason, and he flees and escapes, his siblings, his wife, his family, and his kinsmen who are living, those who did no harm, shall not be harmed in any oppressive or ruinous way.

AUGUST 26, 1828

125 2–Himaka nitak pilla ma, kvna hocha yvmichi bvnna keyu hosh; pilla im isht kvnvpa vlhpiesa hona ahambikmvt vlhto bvt ~~illa hekeyushke~~ [iti vlla hekeyushke] [33]

126 3–Anowa himaka nitak pilla ma yakohmashke: Hat ak vt itibit aha̱shwa tukocha issa tok nana kia; ai yakohmi hokvt achi cha pititi vlli ilahobi hocha ili hi̱bik mvt ilapinli hocha im anukfila hatuk okvt ilap biekvt ituyulot toshbi

125 2–If someone did not intend to do something, but accidentally kills, he will not be punished.

126 3–And from this day forward this article shall be: If men had been fighting each other, and, even though they had quit, and the fighting was feigned, if one kills himself through his own actions, he himself will lie there to decay.

---

33. This section contains eight articles. The first is unnumbered and the rest are numbered from 2 to 7.

hinlashke. **127** Yvmohmikma achvfato ai itivlli ishtvlhpisa hekyushke.

127 Therefore, that other one shall not be held responsible.

128 4–Anonti ilvppa yakoh mashke: Hatak mvt achu̱km ma bvnna nana hokia; nahalupa puta ma ieshi hocha apisalit mihintik ona nana achu̱kma aiahni kvt illi ka bvnna keyu ha tuk okvt nan vbi bvnna, na halupa ieshi ilvppa mihin ti ka fiopa ma i̱ti̱kba i̱ hoko fit kanchi mvto iti vlla he keyushke.

128 4–And this shall be: If a man is in the right, and someone comes straight on holding sharp weapons, since he does not want to die, if he takes the life of the one coming with a weapon, he shall not pay the price.[34]

129 5–Anowa ilvppa yakohmashke

129 5–This shall be:

---

34. This refers to killing in self-defense.

AUGUST 26, 1828

130 kvna fehna hocha yvmichi okma bvnna vlhpiesa hocha hatak itilaui ma fiopa ma, im ihishik mvt aya hekeyushke; itibapishi hoke; imoshi, ibaiyi, i ka nohmi puyuta, ilap itimmi fehna ik nana hatuk okia fiopa ma in tahamblikmvto aya hekeyushke.

131 6–Anowa ilvppa yakohmashke. Hatak tuklo ont atam pa kanohmi hokia itapelvt haksit okla ahantvt hatak achvfa hokia im omvt fiopa ma in tahamblit tuk mvt moma ilap mvt fiopa mvt

130 whoever wants to do right, if he takes away the life of a human being, he shall not be free; his siblings, uncles, nephews and nieces, all kinsmen, all relatives, let it be that if he cuts off their life, he shall not be free.[35]

131 6–This shall be. If a group of two or more men gets out of control, if even one, or all, is killed, all of them shall be executed.

---

35. The person shall be incarcerated.

in tvpa akinlashke.

132 7–Anowa ilvppa yakomash ke—Nana mvt aiokpulo chi hinto tuk ona, hatak fiopa mvto, tahampa chikma isu ba ominili tvshka hieli mvto achukmali pullvt nana ma imvlhtaha achukmvt hielit pihisa akinlashke.

133 Anumpa ma il aiahlichit pin taiyaha hocha anumpa hatukmvno—pi hochifo ha e lapalihinchishke—
   Iahokatvbi ×
   Holvbi ×
   Miashambi ×
   Pistembi
   Hakluntvbi ×

132 7–This amendment shall be—The authorized lighthorsemen shall carefully scrutinize the most serious criminal cases, when one is to be put to death.

133 We have completed the establishment of these laws—we attach our names here—

AUGUST 26, 1828

Koihvmma × Kamiti	Committee
Hushishi humma ×	
Jeremiah Folsom ×	
PP Pitchlynn—	
Benjamin James	
Robert Folsom—	
Lewi Folsom Ahepvtuklo iMiko vt aiokpvchi aiahlichishke	Levi Folsom Chief of the Ahepvtukla approves
Im oklvsha Hopaii	The tribal shamans
Pitama Hopaii Hopaii Hopaii Iskitini	Shamans
Chahta Ahepvtukla	Choctaw Ahepvtukla
Akvs 26 1828	August 26, 1828

134 Nana ka anumpa mvt

134 If the law is written erroneously, widows and orphans shall be deprived of their inheritance.

9

ikachumkmot ashuchikvt
takalikma, ohoyo vlhtakla,
vlla vlhtakla puta mvno,
a wihinli he.   **135** Yvmohmi
chatuk nana kia anum-
pa kamvssa mvno him-
             il ikbit
aka nitak fehna kvno ~~il vht~~
il apihisvshke   a
~~chikbishke~~   **136** Himak nitak
pilla mano yakohmashke.

137 Nakni ahanta kvto nana
ma, apesa mvto ik in
taiyaho hatuk ocha illi
mvt kvniak ma, nan
vlhpoa, imvlayak puyuta
hatuk vt, tekchi: imvlla
yvmohmi hona immi hashke.

135 We will make and ratify a stronger law on this day at this time.

136 From now on, this is the way it will be.

137 When a man dies without having made a will, his wife and his children shall come to inherit all his lifestock and estate.

AUGUST 26, 1828

138 Yvmohmikmvt ohoyo vlhtakla hokvt ihatak vt-tok im ilayalak atuk a kvshapa ituyula tuchinakma **139** ohoyo yaya hatuk vt okchaya itin takla kakosh kvshapa achvfa kvt immi hashke: amba kvshapa tuklo kvto vlla immihashke. **140** Yohmi kia vlla mvt iksho hatukma hatak illi tok ikanohmi ho-cha ibbak ma fokka ahinlashke.

141 2-Anowa yakohmashke - kvna hocha nana apesa mvt i hatak, tekchi, kani mampo kvto nanvlhpisa achukma mvto, ik imiksho[36]

138 And so, the widow shall inherit her husband's property divided into three portions.

139 While the grieving woman is alive she shall own one part: but the children shall inherit two parts.

140 However, if the man died without children, his relatives can inherit.

141 2-This shall be the law—if someone, either husband or wife has no will—

---

36. *Nanvlhpisa achukma ik imiksho* means 'to lack a will', or to be intestate.

19th

hocha,—~~yvmma imilayak atukvt~~—

142 kanimampo hokia illikma, yvmma im il-ayak atuk vt kvshapa tuchi-na itulakma itauwa tuk vt itihullot achukmvt ahashwa na hvshi ona ushta ona hatukma   143 im ilayak kvshapa achvfa yvmmak ona nakni osh illi tukma, kvshapa achvfa ilvppako ohoyo hvt ishash ke

144 Yvmohmik ma ohoyo hosh illi tukma nakni okvt kvshapa achvfa kako ishi makinlik ma peh

142 so, if either one dies, that property shall be divided into three parts if they were living together compatibly for four months;

143 regarding the property that they had during this time, when the man should die, the woman shall get this one part.

144 And so, when the woman should die, the man shall in the same way get one portion

tahlaklaka itilauikma: both being treated equally: **145** but two parts shall be put in the hands of relatives.

145 amba kvshapa tuklo hokvto ihinli tok ilvppa i kanohni hona ibbak ma fokka akinlashke.

146 3-Yvmohmikmvt anonti ilvppa yakohmashke. Kvna hocha nana ma apesa mvto intaiyaha cha illi mvt kvniakma anumpa nana hona ai apihisa pulla tukmvt mihi ocha aiahlit fullotashke. **147** Ik yvmohmi nana kia kvnafehna hocha im ohoyo, im vlla puta: yvmohmikmvt a tahlaklaka mika kvt nana

146 3–And so, if someone dies and he has indeed prepared a properly documented will, wherein the parties are in agreement, the terms of the will shall be fulfilled.

147 However, let it be that every individual's will must provide for his wife and children, both of them;

apihisa kvt ilap im vlla tuk
mvto nanaka ik ahobo kahe
nana ma apihisa tuk ma
yvmmak okvto anumpa
mvt ik aiahlo kashke.

148 Yakohmashke vlla: ishki:
iki hokmá akaninampo
hokvt ilvppa illi tok im il-
ayaka iklvnna halvllashke.

149 Amba vlla kia iksho hatuk
mvno; nana imilayak ka-
shapa itula tuchina ka,
kvshapa achvfa ka, ohoyo
hokma, nakni okma, kani-
mampo hocha okchaya hok
mvt kvshapa achvfa akona

if the will is insufficient for his children, it shall not be upheld.

148 It shall be thus: child, mother, father, any of them, they will get half of the property.

149 But if he has no child, whichever dies, the woman or the man, either, the property will be divided into three parts, either the man or the woman who survives will inherit one part.

AUGUST 26, 1828

ibbak ma f<u>o</u>hkashke **150** Ilvppa in tokowa kakosh hatak illi tok im anumpa mvto ik aiahlokma: amba anum pa inla puta hokvto nana hona ahanchi cha illi mvto kvnia tok ma aiahli bieka fullotashke.

151 4–Ilvppakona il anumpa honlishke. Ilvppa chim ilayak nana puta chimmi ka a svlli hocha sakvniak ma ilvppa hioke. **152** Ish aiah nikmvt, hatak ithana a-chukma nakni <u>a</u>hli a-chukma kvna ilvppa feh

150 If there is no properly verified will, other documents may be used to bring about the deceased's statement before he died.

151 4–At this point in time we shall continue deliberating. After my death and my passing, all the property that is yours shall be this way. **152** If you wish, a well-educated good man[37] shall be present

---

37. For instance, a lawyer.

nvshke; **153** achit chim taiya hvt chilli tukma, anumpa mvto aiahleshke.   **154** Nana chim anukfila ha holisso nana kia ish o̱bohlit ish taiyahli cha chilli tukma anumpa yvmmvt aiahli makinla himak oke.

155 Anumpa ma il aiahli chit pin taiyaha hocha anumpa hatuk mvno pi hohchifo ha e lapalihin chishke
    Iahokahbi ×
    Holvbi ×
    Miashambi ×
    Hakluntvbi ×

153 when you have prepared this statement and died, this will shall be upheld.   **154** Whatever you decide you put on paper, when you have died this will be ratified at this time.[38]

155 Having critiqued this law we attach our names hereby

---

38. The document changes style in this section to address the intended audience in first and second person.

AUGUST 27, 1828

Koihumma Kamiti	Committee
Hushishi humma ×	
Jeremiah Folsom ×	
PP Pitchlynn	
Benjamin James	
Robert Folsom	
Lewi Folsom Ahepvtukla	Levi Folsom Chief of the
i̱ Miko vt aiokpvchi	Ahepvtukla approves
aiahlichishke	
Imoklvsha Hopaii	Tribal shamans
Pitama Hopaii Hopaii	Shamans
Hopaii Iskitini	
Yakni	
Chahta Ahepvtukla	Choctaw Ahepvtukla Country
Akvs 27 1828—	August 27, 1828
156 Yvmohmvshke Kamiti vlheha hatak holitopa puta	**156** And so it is that all the committee members, all the nobles,[39]

---

39. *Hatak holitopa* is used throughout the document and is translated various ways. *Holitopa* has a wide semantic range around the notion of 'esteemed, noble, venerated'.

> 10
> anumpulit e chieya; anumpa il apihisa; anumpa pim ai achvfvt pin taiyahashke.

> we are seated to deliberate on the law; we shall prepare it and we shall all be in unison.

157 Himaka nitak pilla ma nahullo nipi tohbi hvt Chahta ohoyo—itawaya chikmvt, ulhti achvfa ilvppa hatak miko ahanta: mihiona holisso ma ihohowa na holisso atukma hatak holitopa mvto ibbak ma fohoki;

157 From this day forward, when a white man and a Choctaw woman marry, an officer of the particular district will be present; at the same time the marriage license must be put in the hands of an official.[40]

158 Yvmohmikmvt vba numpa ishtika keyu hokmvt hatak ohoyo itawaiyacha he vlhtohoka tuk ona mihio

158 And so, if the marriage is not done in a religious ceremony, the man and woman can officially marry

---

40. Here hatak holitopa can mean either a minister or someone not religiously affiliated.

kanimampo kvto im a-
numpuli mvto in taiyaha
hona itim onvt itauwaya
makinlashke **159** Ayvmohmit
taiyahakma hatak pibafohka
hocha pia holhtiena hioke.

160 2-Yvmohmishke anowa
anumpa ilvppa apesvt
pim achahafvshke.

161 Himaka nitak pilla ma,
Nahullo mvto Chahta ohoyo
atukma itauwa ik nanakia
ohoyo im ilayak atukma
ohoyo mvto vlhpiesa; aiahni
keyu ka i kanchit isht ik
i yopomo kashke.

either by official word or religious ceremony, both are valid.

159 And thus, the man will be included with us and be counted with us.

160 2-And so it shall be that we shall all be in agreement with the law.

161 From this day forward, if a white man and Choctaw woman are married, the woman has a right to their property; they cannot sell it frivolously if they are not in agreement.

162 Yvmohmikmvt yakohmashke Nahullo hvt ohoyo ma itauwaya tuk ocha peh pilla fehna kanchit apis anlit im anukfilvt taiyaha cha maya chikma nana ma tekchi atukma im olvbbi makinlashke—

163 Ulhti ilvppa kamiti ahashwa; hatak an umpuli itapeha ahashwa mvto yvmma vhli hona chilofa makinlashke; ahan chikma ~~mioh~~ mihi ocha aiahlashke.

164 Yvmohmikmvt nan itauwayvt achukma atukvt ilapinli hocha

162 And it shall be decreed that when a white man and a woman have been married, if the man decides to sell the property precipitously, the wife shall be restricted from doing so.

163 This council's present combined committee will come to an end and be in recess; if this is decided and approved.

164 And so it is that this joint session, which has been positive,

hokofa pulla hokvt hatak il itiba holhtena tuk vt i̱ hokofa makinlashke.

165 3-Anonti anumpa ilvppa pim anukfilvt pim aiachvf vt pin taiyahashke—

166 Nahullo nipi tohbi mvto Chahta ohoyo hoka itauwaya tuk ona, ohoyo mvto illit kvni akma, ohoyo immi hatuka i̱ hatak atuk mvt ishit Chahta okla ha isht a kochit kanima isht ikaiyo ka himak oke—

167 Yvmohmikmvt vno akinli kvt nana hona akkvnichi ik aiahni nana kia nana ma kvnicha hekeyushke.

must be in recess and it has been voted unanimously to recess.

165 3-And our deliberations have come to a conclusion—

166 If a white man is married to a Choctaw woman, if that woman is deceased, the woman's possessions cannot be taken out of the Choctaw nation and taken away—

167 And thus he shall have no recourse.

168 4–Anowa ilvppa ik yvm ohmo kashke—aiahnit pim anumpa mvt it imachvfvt apesvt e taiyahlishke.

169 Himaka pilla ma nahullo nipi tohbi mvto ilvppa pi takla ahanta kvt ohoyo mvt intuklo; vlhpesa hekeyushke.   170 Amba ohoyo mvt achvfa itauwaya hocha anumpa mvto im aiahla he mak oke.   171 Yvmma cheyuhmi; himaka nitak pilla mvno—inla mak kia ohoyo achvfa hona itauwaya he ona peh yohmi ik bano il aiahnishke.

168 4–This article shall be operative—We must decide this law to be finalized unanimously.

169 From now on, that white man who is living among us, who has two wives; this is not legal.

170 However, if he is married to one woman, that shall be lawful.

171 With respect to that, we have decided that from this day forward all the rest shall have only one wife.

AUGUST 27, 1828

172 Anumpa ma il aiahlichit pin taiyaha hocha anum pa hatukmvno pi hohchifo ka e lapalihinchishke.
    Iahokatvbi ×
    Holvbi ×
    Miashambi ×
    Pistembi
    Hakluntvbi ×
    Koi humma ×
    Hushishi humma ×
    J. Folsom
    PP Pitchlynn
    Benjamin James
    Robert Folsom
    Lewi Folsom Ahepvtukla i miko vt aiokpvchit aiahlichishke

172 We have finalized this law and we hereby attach our names.

Levi Folsom Chief of the Ahepvtukla approves

Imoklvsha Hopaii / Tribal shamans
Pitema Hopaii Hopaii / Shamans
Hopaii Iskitini
Yakni
Chahta Ahepvtukla / Choctaw Ahepvtukla Country
Akvs 27 1828 / August 27, 1828

173 Yvmohmishke Komiti vhleha hatak holitopa puta anumpulit chiiya, anumpa il apih̠isa; anumpa mvt pim ai achvfvt pin taiyahashke.

173 And so members of the Committee, authorized men selected to pass laws, we shall have come together to ratify these laws.

174 Himak a nitak pilla ona kvna hocha hatak itilaui ka haksobish oka bvshli kopoli hokma nana hocha yvmi chit im okpahanikmvt tvli holisso pokoli vlhpisa ho na im atobbashke.

174 From this day forward, any human being who bites someone's ear off and causes him harm shall be fined the appropriate amount of money.

175 Yvmma

175 If he cannot pay the fine, he shall be flogged ten lashes with a switch, without clothes, on his bare back.

AUGUST 27, 1828

ik atobbokmvt ilefoka kia iksho, nvli bieka hona iti tvpa mvto fahama pokoli onvtahonla makinlashke.

176 Anowa ilvppa il apihisa anumpa mvt aiachvf vt pin taiyahvshke. Hatak itilaui ma nishkin kia kahlali; im okpvni, yvmichi kvt, peh yvmichi bvnna vlhpiesa hosh yvmihinchik ma tvli holisso vlhpisa mvt pokoli tuchina akocha mvt tahlapi aiena hona isht im atobbi makinlashke—

177 Yvmma keyukma iti tvpa mvto fahama pokoli tuchina

176 We have unanimously ratified this amendment. Any individual who deliberately scratches out the eye of another, harming him, and it was premeditated, he shall be fined the appropriate amount of thirty-five dollars

177 Or, if not, he shall receive thirty-five

11

akocha tahlapi kash ocha onvtohonlikma nana im aiokpulo tuk vt nuktvlvt binila hina hoke.

lashes until the victim has been appeased.

178 Anumpa ma il aiahli chit pin taiyaha hocha anumpa hatuk mvno pi hohchifo ka e lapalihinchishke.

    Iahokatvbi ×
    Holvbi ×
    Miashambi ×
    Pistembi ×
    Hakluntvbi ×
    Koi humma ×
    Hushishi humma ×
    Jeremiah Folsom ×
    PP Pitchlynn
    Benjamin James
    Robert Folsom

178 We have come to our decision about these laws and hereby attach our names.

AUGUST 28, 1828

Lewi Folsom Ahepvtukla
   i Miko vt aiohpv
   chi aiahlichishki
Imoklvshi Hopaii
Pitema Hopaii Hopaii
Hopaii Iskitini
   Yakni
Chahta Ahepvtukla
   Akvs 28 1828

Levi Folsom Chief of the
Ahepvtukla approves

Tribal Shamans
Shamans

Choctaw Aheptukla Country
   August 28, 1828

179 Yvmohmvishke Kamiti vhleha, hatak holitopa vlheha; anumpulit e chiya; an umpa il apihisa; anumpa mvt pim aiachvfvt pin tai yahashke.

179 And so the Committee members, the authorized men, are in session. We shall be ratifying these amendments together.

180 Yvmohmishke Himak a

180 And so, from this day forward the particular district shall appoint someone to care for stray horses.

     achvfa
nitak pilla ma ulhti ^ il
vppa fehnaka isuba kvn
ia puta ka potohonla hi-
vt vlhtokashske **181** Yvmoh
mikmvt isuba kvnia
puta ka achukmalit it
ahobashke **182** Yvmohmik
mvt isuba kanohmi
hatukma achukmalit
anohonlikmvt, hishi kanioh
mi; isht i̱ chuwa aiena kvt
lapali hokma anumpa ma
ikbit anohonlashke. **183** Yvmoh
mit taiyaha nana kia ilap
atukmvt nanvlhpoa ma
ont ik hoyo hona hvshi tuklo

181 And this person shall carefully corral all the stray horses.

182 Therefore, he shall make a description—he shall carefully identify the number of horses, the color of their coats, and if they have a brand on them.

183 After all this, if the owner of the animal does not come to look for and claim it in two months

AUGUST 28, 1828

vlhpiesat ont ataiyahakma isuba hatukmvto, hatak laua pisa hona nanvlh toba makinlashke **184** Hvshi hvnali atobba he ocha nan vlhpoa mvno ishi makinslashke: **185** Yvmohmik ma im isuba hvt tok mvto hvshi hanali ai iti tahlaka akostininchit ik ai eshokma chumpa tuk vt isuba mvto immi aiahli tobashke **186** Tvli holisso ilvppa nan vlhpoa ita ahombi tukvt ulhti talaia tvli holisso ai it uyula achukmvt itula mak inlashke **187** Yvmohmik ma

the expenses of the horse's care shall be put into public notice.

184 Someone must pay expenses for six months and then may take the animal.

185 Someone who has paid for the horse's feeding has a lien on the horse. And so, with respect to the horse, if the owner does not claim it within six months, the one who has paid has bought the horse; it shall become his.

186 The money that was collected for the animal by the district will be banked[41] by the district.

187 And so the person who provided the description of the animal shall be paid a fee of one dollar.

---

41. *Ai ituyula achukmvt* is literally to 'lay it down well' or put the money in a safe place.

nanvlhpoa kvnia ishit
anumpa puta ma kahpa
honli tukvt tvli holisso a
chvfa im vlhtoba makinlashke

188 Anonti ilvppa yakohmashke
Hatak nanvlhtoka ilvppvt
isuba achukma nana ho po
tohonlik mvt isuba toksvli
imma hok mak bano—achuk-
malit isuba ma ilbvshala
he keyu ho hatak a ibbak ma
fohkikma, isuba toksvli an
ta kvt impa ka itilatobbi
makinlashke **189** Amba yvmma
keyu hokma achukmvt
lumit hikia Tanchi puta
vpa hocha hikiakma, nitak

188 And also, the appointed animal handler,[42] if he has a good workhorse, he should put it in the hands of a man who won't abuse it; for this workhorse shall pay for its own feeding.

189 But if that is not the case, and it is placed in a stall and eats a lot of corn,

---

42. This would be like a stableman.

AUGUST 28, 1828

      ka
hullo achvfa tvli holisso a-
chvfa vlhtoba hocha ieshke.

190 Anumpa ma il aiahli-
chit pin taiyaha hocha-
anumpa hatukmvno pi
hohchifo ka e lapalihinchishke
    Iahokatvbi ×
    Holvbi ×
    Miashambi ×
    Pistembi ×
    Hakluntvbi ×
    Koi humma ×
    Hushishi humma ×
    Jeremiah Folsom ×
    PP Pitchlynn
    Benjamin James
    Robert Folsom

its fee will be one dollar a week.

190 We have come to our conclusion with passing this law and we hereby attach our names.

Records of the Choctaw Council Meetings

Lewi Folsom Ahepvtuklo
  i miko vt aiokpvchi
aiahlichishke
Im oklvsha Hopaii
Pitema Hopaii   Hopaii
Hopaii Iskitini
  Yakni
  Chahta Ahepvtukla
  Akvs 28 1828

191 Himaka nitak fehna kvno Kamiti puta, hatak holitopa vlheha aiena hocha e chiyvt nan apihisvt pim hvppin aiachvfvt taiyahashke

192 Himaka nitak pilla na holihta vto chaha kvt iyi tahlapi hocha holihta vt ai ahlashke.   **193** Holihta aiahli

Levi Folsom Chief of the Ahepvtukla approves

Tribal Shamans
Shamans

  Choctaw Ahepvtukla Country
  August 28, 1828

191 On this very day the Committees and important noblemen are in session to ratify and pass laws.

192 From this time forward, fences shall be at the height of five feet.

193 One will be fined if livestock cross this fence and destroy it.

AUGUST 28, 1828

yvmohmi ka nanvlhpoa
kvto osapa tukmvno chuk
oh̲owakma nana okpo-
honlo kvto im vlhtoba makinlashke.   194 Nanvlhpoa yvm
ma nana okpahani tok
im pushnayo makash i̲
~~kvnik~~ kvnikma himak oke

194 The owner of the animals that destroy something will be held responsible.

195 Anowa ilvppa yakohma
hi ona anumpa mvto
   hvppin
pim aiachvfvt taiyahashke

195 We all agree on this amendment.

196 Himak a nitak pilla ma
holihta osapa apakfoyupa
kvto holihta vt abana aka
fehna ai itonlvut [aivlot]
itvbanit vba ia kvt iyi
tuklo, tuchina chaha

196 From this day forward a fence that surrounds a field will be built two to three feet high.

12

yvmma **197** aialaka holih ta itvbana itintakla ho kvt chiluk vt ibbak ishki itontuvla ushta hocha ho lihta mvto holihta aiahlihashke. **198** Yvmohmi hona shukha nana kia holihta yvmohmi kvno—hlipohonli nana okpahanikma, nana vlhpoa yvmma chiyuhmi immi ahanta kvto nana okpahani ka nan ikvnikia makinlashke.

199 Yvmohmikma kvpi tvni hatak pehlichi ilaiyuka hocha hatak a pehlichi mvto

197 The space in between (the logs) will be four inches.

198 If a hog goes through the fence and destroys it, the one who owns the animal will be held responsible.

199 Therefore each captain and the men who lead

AUGUST 28, 1828

binilit fullota kvt achukmalit pullvt nana puta
kano anumpa ilvppa
vlhpihisa ka apesvt aia
hlicha himak ocha nana
apesvchi kvto aiahanta
makinlashke

    Iahokatvbi ×
    Holvbi ×
    Miashambi ×
    Pistembi ×
    Hakluntvbi ×
    Koi humma ×
    Hushishi humma ×
    Jeremiah Folsom ×
    PP Pitchlynn
    Benjamin James
    Robert Folsom

are seated, the majority are in complete agreement and this law shall be passed.

Lewi Folsom Ahepvtukla i Miko vt aiahpvchi aiahlihvshke	Levi Folsom Chief of the Ahepvtukla approves
Imoklusha Hopaii	Tribal Shamans
Pitema Hopaii Hopaii	Shamans
Hopaii Iskitini Yakni	
Chahta Ahepvtukla	Choctaw Ahepvtukla Country
Akvs 28 1828	August 28, 1828

200 Himak nitak fehna kvno Kamiti putta, hatak holitopa vhleha aiena hocha e chieyvt nanapesvt anumpulit anumpa mvto pim ai a chvfvt pin taiyahashke.

201 Himaka nitak pilla ma

200 At this time, all the Committee noblemen are in session together prepared to deliberate and draw up these laws.

201 From now on, the people who are called Choctaw, themselves and others living there, who have been proven to destroy property shall compensate with their own possessions.

August 28, 1828

Chahta okla hona Chahta
hochifo ho na cha aiahanta
tuk ocha ilap bika keyuk-
mvt okla inla piba fohka
keyu ik nana hokia nana
ma im okpahanikmvno
nana okpvni tuk ilvppa fehna
kvno atokowa mvt taiyaha
yvmohmik ma im ilayak
ocha nana ma ishtvlhpisvt
isht chilofa makinlashke.

202 Yvmohmikmvt i kvpi
tvni pulla kvto nana ma
im aiiksiachi makinlashke
Yvmohmi kia kvpitvni
hatuk mvto nana ma im
aiiksiachi ik ithaiyano.

202 And so, he shall make reparations to his own captain, unless his captain does not know how to make reparations.

203 yvmohmikma i shahli hona nana isht ahaiyohonchi mak inlashke

204 Anowa yakohma he il api hisvshke Kvna hocha nana ma nan okpvni mvt a chieto yvmohmi tuk ona iti tvpa nanakia onvtohonla he amo vlhpiesa k~~vno~~ kvpitvni pulla kvto aiahli fehna kvno akosti ninchi makinlashke 205 Yvm ohmi mvto in taiyahakma nana hocha aiahla hetuk mvt aiahli makinlashke

X 206 Anumpa ma il aiahlichit pin taiyaha hocha anumpa ha tukmvno pi hochifo ho e lapali [hinchishke][43]

203 Then, he shall go to his superior.

204 This is what we shall legislate. It shall be that if someone commits a serious crime, he shall be punished by flogging; the captain shall be aware that he has the power to enforce it.

205 This power shall be excercised if it (the accusation) proves to be true.

206 We hereby agree and finalize these amendments and attach our names

---

43. Pitchlynn inserts *amo* to make *kamo* rather than *kvno*. The last syllables are squeezed illegibly onto the page, and we have surmised that they are *hinchishke*.

AUGUST 28, 1828

Iahokatvbi ×
Holvbi ×
Miashambi ×
Pistembi ×
Hakluntvbi ×
Koi humma ×
Hushishi humma ×
Jeremiah Folsom ×
PP Pitchlynn
Benjamin James
Robert Folsom

Lewi Folsom Ahepvtukla
    i miko vt aiokpvc
    chit aiahlishke
	Levi Folsom Chief of the
	Ahepvtukla approves

Imoklvsha Hopaii	Tribal Shamans
Pitema Hopaii	Shamans
Hopaii Iskitini	

Yakni
Chahta Ahepvtukla
Akvs 28 1828

Choctaw Ahepvtukla Country
August 28, 1828

207 Himaka nitak fehna kvno Kamiti puta, hatak holitopa vhleha aiena hocha e chieyvt nanapesvt anumpulit anumpa mvto pin aiachv fvt pintaiyahashke

207 At this time, the Committee and noblemen are in session, prepared to review laws, deliberate on them, and agree on them.

208 Himak a nitak pilla ma yvmohma heona il apihisvshke.

208 Hence, we shall legislate.

209 Hatak tuchina foka hocha ulhti achvfa ilvppa vlhtoka kvto wak kvnia puta mihi ona ibbak ma fohka makin lashke

209 Around three men from a particular district [44] are authorized to take charge of stray cattle.

210 Yvmohmik mvt hv shi tuchina itintaiyakla kako

210 It is necessary to present a claim within three months.

---

44. The district in which they reside.

AUGUST 28, 1828

anumpa mvno kahpulli hokvto tahli pullashke. **211** Wak mvt yvmohmi; isht ichuwa mvt yvmohmi achit ano honlashke.

211 The cow must be identified by its brand.

212 Yvmohmi na hvshi tuchina kvto nana anowa tukvt ont taiyahakma ilap atuk mvto nan vlhpoa kvno ant ik hoyokma hatuk lawa a chukma pisa hona nana iti vlli makinlashke. **213** Nan chuhumpa kvt nan i kvnia moma i shayahli hocha aiahlashke

212 After three months of public notice, if no one has come to claim the animal, it will be put into public view so a price can be offered.

213 All the strays will be sold to the one with the highest bid,

214 ik yomohmi nana kia nan vlhpoa impushnayo vt tok vt nan iti vlli tok yvmma fehna

214 but if the animal's owner comes with the exact price

215 a mihintit hvshi hanali
aiona hona ilap vt tok vt
ithaiyanakmvt nan apesa
nan isht im achiba tuk a
in chilofakmvt nanvlhpoa
mvto i̱ falama makinlashke.

215 Anowa yvmohmashke
Nanvlhpoa ilvppa tvli ho
lisso ~~tvli holisso~~ vlhtohomba
tok. tvli holisso ilvppa ituyula kvt ulhti achvfa il-
vppa tvli holisso aiitola
     u
yona ituyu̶la makinlashke.

216 Anowa yakohmashke.
Nana ma im achiebvt
nan vlhpoa kvnia ilvppa
potohonlit im achiebvt

215 at the end of six months, he will pay the delayed charges to the bidders and the animal will be returned to him.[45]

215 And so this shall be the amendment.
This stock will continue to be paid for. The money will be held[46] and will remain in the particular district where it is banked.

216 This shall be the amendment. The one who has taken the trouble in handling the stray stock

---

45. This seems to describe a lien.
46. As if the money were in escrow.

AUGUST 28, 1828

nana ma isht atohombit
im achieba tuk vt wak a-
chvfat ia ka iskvli ushta
  × vlhtobvt
hocha im ~~atobvt~~ ibbak ma
fohkashke—

217 Anumpa ma il aihli-
chit pin taiyah hocha
anumpa hatukmvno—
pi̱ hohchifo ha e lapali
hinchishke
  Iahokatvbi ×
  Holvbi ×
  Miashambi ×
  Pistembi ×
  Hakluntvbi ×
  Koi humma ×
  Hushi̱shi humma ×

will be paid for his effort for each of the cattle, four dollars shall be placed in his hands.

217 We agree and conclude by attaching our names.

Jeremiah Folsom ×
PP Pitchlynn
Benjamin James
Robert Folsom

Lewi Folsom Ahepvtukla i miko vt aiokpvchit aiahlichishke	Levi Folsom Chief of the Ahepvtukla approves
Imoklvsha Hopaii	Tribal Shamans
Pitema Hopaii	Shamans
Hopaii Iskitini Yakni	
Chahta Ahepvtukla	Choctaw Ahepvtukla Country
Akvs 28 1828	August 28, 1828
218 Kamiti vhleha, hatak ho litopa puta mvto Chun nitak ont ishtauatuklo minvt[47] 1827—yvmma nitak fehna	218 The Committees, the important men have read and approved the minutes of the June 12, 1827, meeting, that exact day.

---

47. *Minvt* is borrowed from the English 'minutes'.

AUGUST 28, 1828

chiya hocha anumpa
mvto im aiachvfvt tai
yaha kvt yakahanchi tok oke.

219 Hatak nana hocha ohoyo nowvt aya kvno—i bvnna keyu hona hoklit okpaiyani na anumpa mvto atokowvt taiyahakma iti tvpa mvto ilefoka kia iiksho nvli bi-eka, yvmohmi hona faha ma mvto pokoli tuchina akocha tahlapi onvtula himak ona 220 anumpa mvto vlhpihisa kv-mo.

221 Anowa ilvppa fehna ka achakaya ma ilapihisvshke

222 Himaka nitak pilla ma ohoyo

219 If any man visits a woman and without her consent rapes her, and if this is proven, he will receive thirty-five lashes on his bare back, without clothes.

220 This law is being passed and it is just.

221 We add this amendment.

222 Henceforth, any important woman[48] who lies and charges a man with rape, if it's proven that the woman has been lying, the liar shall receive twenty-five lashes on the bare back.

---

48. *Ohoyo nana fehna* incontrovertibly means 'important woman'.

nana fehna hocha holabit
nakni oka onohonchi mvto
hatak ilvppvt ai hoklit ai ok
pahanishke; achi nanakia
peh holabi hocha anumpa
mvno—onochi vlhpiesa ha
tukma ohoyo holabi ilvppa
anumpa mvto aiahlit ato-
kowa mvto taiyaha; yvm
ohmi tuk a ilefoka kia ik
sho. nvli bieka hona iti tvpa
mvto fahama pokoli tuklo
akocha tahlapi nvli atuk
mvno onvtula makinlashke.

223 Yakohmashke i̱ kvpitvni keyukmvt isuba ominili tvshka kanima hokia fvma

223 And so the captain or the lighthorsemen will carry out the sentence.

AUGUST 28, 1828

224 Anumpa ma il aiahlichi
pin taiyaha hocha anumpa
hatuk mvno pi hochifo ha
e lapalihinchishke—
    mvno aiahlichi makinlashke
    Iahokatvbi ×
    Holvbi ×
    Miashambi ×
    Pistembi ×
    Haklontvbi ×
    Koi humma ×   Kamiti
    Hvshishi humma ×
    Jeremiah Folsom ×
    PP Pitchlynn
    Benjamin James
    Robert Folsom

224 We have agreed on this
amendment and have attached
our names—

Committee

Lewi Folsom Ahepvtukla miko vt aiopv chit aiahlichiske	Levi Folsom Chief of the Ahepvtukla approves
Imoklvsha Hopaii	Tribal Shamans
Pitema Hopaii Hopaii	Shamans
Hopaii Iskitini Yakni	
Chahta Ahepvtukla	Choctaw Ahepvtukla Country
Akvs 28th 1828	August 28th, 1828

225 Himak nitak fehna kvno Kamiti puta, hatak holitopa vhleha aiena hocha e chieyvt nanapesvt anumpulit an umpa mvto pim aiachvfvt pin taiyahashke—

225 On this very day, we the Committees and authorized men are in session to deliberate on and pass legislation.

226 Himaka nitak pilla ma,

226 Henceforth, if someone employs someone to steal someone else's property, and if this is confirmed, the man who was the instigator shall be equally guilty as the one who stole.

AUGUST 28, 1828

kvna fehna hokia nana ho ka h<u>u</u>kopa hi ona inla ya toh<u>o</u>no na hatak im ilayak oka huh<u>u</u>kopakma, hatak ilvppa fehna nana tohno tok ona, anumpa mvto atokowvt ai yahakma,   **227** hatak im ilayak kvniohmi hocha im anumpa pulla hona im anumpa pulla hona, nana mvto ok punlo ~~mvto~~ kvno chilofa makinlashke.   **228** Yvmohmik mvt hatak ilvppa h<u>u</u>kopa tok, aiena toh<u>o</u>no tok itatuklo ka hatak nanapesa chieya kvto ilvppa fehna hona nahaksi tok okvt nana ha yvmohmi hona ~~aiishit~~ a ishit hotopah makinlashke.

227 The penalty will be the value of the property according to the word of the victim.

228 And so a sitting judge shall punish both the thief and the one who hired him. Hence, the one who was duped, having done such a thing, shall be punished.

---

49. The "one who was duped" is the thief.

14

229 Itilaui hocha anumpa mvto atokowashke

230 Anumpa ma il aiahlichit pin taiyaha hocha anumpa hatukmvno pi hochifo ha e lapalihinchishke—

    Iahokatvbi ×
    Holvbi ×
    Miashambi ×
    Pistembi ×
    Hakluntvbi ×
    Koi hvmma ×
    Hushishihumma ×
    Jeremiah Folsom ×
    PP Pitchlynn
    Benjamin James
    Robert Folsom

229 This will apply equally and definitely.

230 We are in agreement on this amendment and so attach our names—

AUGUST 28, 1828

Lewi Folsom Ahepvtukla i mi ko vt aiokpvchit ai ahlichishke

Levi Folsom Chief of the Ahepvtukla approves

Im oklvshi Hopaii
Pitema Hopaii   Hopaii
Hopaii Iskitini
    Yakni
    Chahta Ahepvtukla
    Akvs 28th 1828

Tribal Shamans
Shamans

    Choctaw Ahepvtukla Country
    August 28th, 1828

a fehna

231 Himak ^ nitak kvno—kamiti puta, hatak holitopa vlheha ai ena hocha e chieyvt nanapesvt anumpulit anumpa mvto pim aiachvfvt pin taiyahishke.

231 On this very day, the committees, the important men, are seated to deliberate and agree on these laws.

232 Himaka nitak pilla ma kvna hokia hatak ahanta it

232 From this day forward, if any person

ilaui ka nana a kvniohmi ai isht hotopa he a chinto fullota hona holabi hocha aiahliha fehnaho anoh*o*chikma, holabi kvto aiahli bieka, anumpa mvto alotowvt taiyahakma iti tvpa mvto—fahama pokoli tahlapi hocha ilefoka kia iksho hona nvli atuk mvno—onvtohon la makinlashke.

commits great harm through lying, if the lying is verified, he will be charged and when the decision has been finalized,[50] he will receive fifty lashes on the bare back.

233 Anumpa ma il aiahlichit pin taiyaha hocha anumpa hatukmvno p*i* hochifo ha e lapalihinchishke

    Iahokatvbi ×
    Holvbi ×
    Miashambi ×

233 We have decided on this amendment and hereby attach our names

---

50. The judge, jury, or other body has ruled.

AUGUST 28, 1828

Pistembi ×
Hakluntvbi ×
Koi humma ×
Hushishi humma ×
Jeremiah Folsom ×
PP Pitchlynn
Benjamin James
Robert Folsom—

Lewi Folsom Ahepvtukla i miko vt aiokpvchit aiahlichishke	Levi Folsom Chief of the Ahepvtukla approves
Im oklvsha Hopaii	Tribal Shamans
Pitema Hopaii Hopaii	Shamans
Hopaii Iskitini	
Yakni	
Chahta Ahepvtukla	Choctaw Ahepvtukla Country
Akvs 28 1828	August 28, 1828

234 Himaka nitak fehna kvno Kamiti puta, hatak holitopa vhleha aiena hocha e chieyvt nanapesvt anumpulit anumpa mvto pim aia chvfvt pin taiyahvshke

235 Yakohmashke. Himaka nitak pilla ma kvna fehna ho cha anumpa vlhpisa ma ik aiokpachot hot nana ma haksit ahanta; yvmohmit ahanta cha isuba o minili tvsh ka vhleha hokvt anumpa vlhpisa ilvppa aiahlichi hocha aya kvno, 236 kvna fehna hokia kvniohmit ahantvt okpulot

234 On this very day the Committees, important men, we are in session to deliberate and come to unanimous agreement on these laws.

235 It shall be thus. In the future, if someone disagrees with these laws and becomes disorderly and continues so, and if this person becomes violent toward a lawman in the performance of his legal duty

236 the law states that if even one lawman is somehow killed in the line of duty, the captain will be summoned at his residence, and the brigade will be raised.

AUGUST 28, 1828

isuba o manili tvshka anumpa ma aioklhilichi hocha aya fehna hona isuba o mi nili tvshka ya achvfonakia nakvnichit aiyabikma hatak kvpitvni yvmma aiahanta fehna hona, ai yvmohmikma; intvshka pehlinchit wakaya hioke.

237 Yvmohmikmvt isuba o mi nili tvshka tukma ai itvpe lishchi hocha nana okpahani tuka fiopa mvno in tvblit kanchi pulla hocha achukmvt hieleshke—

237 And so if the lawman is containing a harmful situation and it is necessary to take a life, he will be justified.

238 Anumpa ma il aiahlichit pin taiyaha hocha anumpa

238 This law has been ratified and concluded.

hatuk mvno—pi̱ hochifo ha we attach our names
e lapalihinchishke—
Iahokatvbi ×
 Holvbi ×
 Miashambi
 Pistembi ×
 Hakluntvbi ×
 Koihumma × Kam
 Hushi̱shi humma ×
 Jeremiah Folsom ×
 PP Pitchlynn
 Benjamin James
 Robert Folsom
 Lewi Folsom Ahepvtukla Levi Folsom Chief of the
  i miko vt aiokpa Ahepvtukla approves
  chit aiahlishke
Im oklusha Hopaii Tribal Shamans
Pistema Hopaii Hopaii Shamans
Hopaii Iskitini

AUGUST 29, 1828

Yakni
Chahta Ahepvtukla
Akvs 29 1828

Choctaw Ahepvtukla Country
August 29, 1828

239 Himaka nitak fehnahona Kamiti puta, hatak holitopa vhle ha aiena hocha e chieyvt ~~on in~~ nanpesvt anumpulit anumpa mvto pim aiachvfvt pin taiyahashke.

239 On this very day, all the Committees and honorable men, we are in session to agree upon and conclude these laws.

240 Himaka nitak pilla ma ik yvmohmo ka hiona anumpa mvto pim achvfvt pin taiyahvshke.

240 From this time forward, we shall be in agreement that the following shall be prohibited.

241 Hatak lusa yuka hoka, Chahta okla mikmvt nipi tohbi vhleha Chahta holhtena itea ~~hochifo~~ kvto itauwaya he keyushke.

241 Choctaw people and the white people who are counted with the Choctaws[51] shall not marry black slaves.

242 Aiahnit apesa mvt pintaiyahashke.

242 We have concluded that this is our decision.

---

51. White people of whatever status who live among the Choctaws.

243 Anowa yakohmashke—
Kvna fehna hocha hatak lusa
yuka im ahashwa kvt hatak
vpi humma: keyukmvt nipi
tohbi; kanimampo hokia, hatak
lusa im ahashwa kvt, ik yvm
ohmi aiahnit aiokpahanchi
hona— **244** Kvna hocha
akostini-
chit anohonli na anumpa
mvto aiahlit atohonvt taiyahakma; tvli holisso pokoli tahlapi
kvto i kvnihiakma; iklvnna
hokvt nana akostinichi yvmma
fehna tuka—iklvnna kvt ibbak
fohkakma; anowa—iklvnna
kvshapa kvt Ahepitukla ulh
ti tvli holisso ai itolah vlh

243 This shall be the article—
Whoever owns black slaves,
Indian or white, whichever it may
be, let the one who owns black
people hope it does not happen.[52]

244 If someone reliably finds out and
reports this, and it is proven,
the owner will be fined fifty
dollars, half will be placed in the
hands of the witness, and half
will be placed in the Ahepvtukla
government account.

---

52. Relations or marriage between Choctaws or whites and slaves.

This photograph of pages 96–97 of the journal shows its typical handwriting style and organization. Reprinted by permission from Western History Collections, University of Oklahoma Libraries.

piesa kvno achukmvt ituyula makinlashke.

245 Anowa yakohmashke Hatak vpi humma nakni, mik mvt nipi tohbi yvmohmi ho ite nana ^kia hatak lusa ohoyo yuka hona itauwayakmvt iti tvpa mvto fahama pokoli tuchina akocha mvto tahlapi aiena hocha ilifoka kia iiksho hona nvli atuk mvno ~~ovn~~ vnvtohonla makinlashke.

246 Yvmohmikma anowa yak hi oke ohma~~shke~~ Hatak vpi hvmma ohoyo, nipi tohbi, ite kanimapo hokia hatak lusa yuka hoka auwayakma, iti tvpa mvto

245 The amendment shall be thus. If an Indian man, or a white man, either one, has relations with a black female slave, thirty-five lashes without clothes on will be laid upon his back.

246 And so this amendment shall be. An Indian woman or a white woman, either one, who has intercourse with a black slave

August 29, 1828

fahaha[53] pokoli tuklo akocha mvt tahlapi aiena hocha nvli a onvtola makinlashke.

247 Yvmohmikma nana itau waya ilvppak atukvt im ai issvt it̲i filvmma himakoka

248 Yakohmi tuk ona at̲ukla hona yvmohmik ma nana ishit hotopa mvto vmmona tuka chiyuhmi tuklo kvt vn vtola makinlashke.

249 Anumpa ma ilaiahlichit pin taiyaha hocha anumpa hatukmvno p̲i hohchifo ha e lapalihinchashke
    Iahok̲atvbi ×
    Holvbi ×
    Miashambi ×

will have twenty-five lashes laid upon her back.

247 And then the couple will be separated.

248 And so, for a second time, the punishment of the first time will fall upon both of them.

249 We have ratified this amendment and we attach our names.

---

53. Pitchlynn certainly meant to write *fahama*, 'lashes', here.

Records of the Choctaw Council Meetings

    Pistembi ×
    Hakluntvbi ×
    Koi humma ×
    Hush̲ishi humma ×
    Jeremiah Folsom ×
    PP Pitchlynn
    Benjamamin James
    Robert Folsom

× Lewi Folsom—Ahepvtukla i miko vt aiokpvchit aiahlishke	Levi Folsom—Chief of the Ahepvtukla approves
Imokvshi Hopaii	Tribal Shamans
Pitema Hopaii Hopaii	Shamans
Hopaii Iskitini	
Yakni	
Chahta Ahepvtukla	Choctaw Ahepvtukla Country
Akvs 29 1828	August 29, 1828
250 Himaka nitak fehna kvno—	**250** On this very day, the Committees and honorable men are present and ready to continue to debate and deliberate on these amendments that we shall agree upon.

AUGUST 29, 1828

Kamiti puta, hatak holitopa vhleha aiena hocha e chieyvt nanapesavt anumpulit a-numpa mvto pim aia chvfvt pin taiyahvshke.

251 Himaka nitak pilla ma hatak lusa yuka keyu kvt Chahta okla Ahepvtukla ~~chukocha~~ chukowa cha ahantakma, yvmohmi vlhpiesa he keyu hvt yvmohmishke

252 Il aiahna himakoke. Yvm ohmikma pitakla ahanta he keyushke.

253 Amba kamiti vhleha yvmohmik mvt hatak anumponli anumpulit chiya hocha vlhpiesa im

251 From this day forward those who are not slaves[54] shall not enter and live in the Choctaw Ahepvtukla district proper.

252 This is our decision. They cannot reside among us.

253 But if the committees and authorized persons

---

54. Only Choctaw people and their slaves shall live there.

aiahni hona aiahanta hi
oke Amba vlhpiesa, ik
im aiohnokma anta
hekeyushke.

    Anumpa ma il aiahli
chit pin taiyaha hocha
anumpa hatuk mvno—pi̱
hochifo ha e lapalihinchishke
    Iahokatvbi ×
    Holvbi ×
    Miashambi ×
    Pistembi ×
    Hakluntvbi ×
    Koi humma ×
    Hushi̱shi humma ×
    Jeremiah Folsom ×
    PP Pitchlynn
    Benjamin James
    Robert Folsom

grant permission, someone
may reside there. But if it is not
granted, he cannot.

We have completed these
amendments—we hereby attach
our names.

Lewi Folsom Ahepvtukla i
   miko vt aiokpvchit
   aia̲hlishke
Imoklvsha Hopaii
Pitema Hopaii Hopaii
Hopaii Iskitini
   Yakni
   Chahta Ahepvtukla
   Akvs 29 1828

Levi Folsom Chief of the
Ahepvtukla approves

Tribal Shamans
Shamans

Choctaw Ahepvtukla Country
August 29, 1828

254 Himaka nitak fehna kvno Kamiti puta; hatak holitopa v hleha; aiena hocha e chieyvt nanapesvt anumpulit anumpa mvto aiachvfvt pin taiyahvshke.

254 On this very day, the Committees and the elected people, we are in session to conclude in unison the construction of these laws.

255 Himaka nitak pilla ma yak ohmashke Tvli boli, anowa nana ilaiyuka aiiksiachi im

255 From this day forward, there will be put in place a law that authorizes a professional smith who is skilled in working on all things,

ponvt pi tintakla okla Ahepvtukla, Chahta okla yoka iba takla binili kvt nana vlhpisa mvt yakohmi hona binihinlashke **256** Hatak yvmohmi kvna hocha toh<u>o</u>nokmvt, kamiti vhleha hatak anumponli puta mihiona anumpa vlhpisa aiahlit in taiyahakma nana achukma ahanta kia atoni puta hocha im vlhpiesashke **257** Yvmohmi tuk ona nana mvt ik achukmo—hatak mvt vlhpiesa keyu tuk ona anumpa mvto atokowvt taiyahakma p<u>i</u> yakni atukma a kocha makinlashke.

who is among us Ahepvtukla people, within the Choctaw nation.

256 The ones who hire this person, the same committees and speakers who will finish ratifying this law, are authorized to certify that things are going well.

257 And so if things are not good—if that man is not suitable, if that testimony is proven, that man shall be removed from our property.

AUGUST 29, 1828

258 Anowa yakohmashke—Hatak nana ithana impona: piba fohka ahanta kvt ilvppa ik yvmohmi; aiahnikmvt vpa he vlhpiesa kvt yakni vlhpisa auatuklo foka ka, tan chi awayachikmvt nanvlh poa kia im vlla ai itim vpa he vlhpiesa kvt wayachit apovt ashwa makinlashke.

259 Anumpa ma il aiahlichit pin taiyaha hocha anumpa hatukmvno—pi hochifo ha e lapalihinchishke
- Iahokatvbi ×
- Holvbi ×
- Miashembi ×
- Pistembi ×

258 This shall be the policy—If this is his wish, a professional[55] living among us, so that he has enough to eat, let him be provided with twelve acres so he may raise corn and livestock, and so that he may support his children adequately by raising and producing agricultural products.

259 All being in agreement with this policy, we shall attach our names.

---

55. This may refer to a teacher.

Hakluntvbi ×
Koihumma ×
Hush̲ishi humma ×
Jeremiah Folsom ×
PP Pitchlynn
Benjamin James
Robert Folsom

Lewi Folsom—Ahepvtukla i Miko vt aiahpvchit aiahlichishke	Levi Folsom—Chief of the Ahepvtukla approves
Im oklvsha Hopaii	Tribal Shamans
Pitema Hopaii Hopaii	Shamans
Hopaii Iskitini Yakni	
Chahta Ahepvtukla Akvs 29 1828	Choctaw Ahepvtukla Country August 29, 1828
260 Himaka nitak fehna kvno kamiti puta, hatak holitopa	260 On this very day, the committees and the authorized people, we are in session to deliberate on laws that we shall decide unanimously.

AUGUST 29, 1828

vhleha aiena hocha e chieyvt
nanapesvt anumpulit
anumpa mvto pim aia-
chvfvt pin taiyahashke

261 Himak nitak fehna nana
il apihisa kvt ilvppa fehnvshke

262 Nanilhpitta nana atam
pa afvmmi holhtena mvt
1829—yvmma fehna aya
he tuka nana isht il apesa
kvt ilvppak oke. 263 Tvli, Tvlli
kvllo: tvli aboa hi; yvmohmikmvt
tvli boli: nana a isht im vlh
toba hi; mikmvt kashapa
chiyvhmi kvt ponola ashana
yohmi kia ai isht akancha
he kia isht il apihisvshke

261 On this very day, the laws that we are constructing shall be final.

262 We shall authorize the expenditures for the excess funds from the year 1829.

263 And so expenditures will be made for metal, tempered metal, a mill, and wages to be paid to a smith; and we shall hereby legislate that some portion shall be given to cotton products,[56] which may be sold.

---

56. Such things as twining and rope.

264 Yvmma chiyuhmi. Hatak miko: kamiti itapeha kvt ahahahni achukma hocha nana ilvppa vlhpisa ha ai-ahlichit nana ma ishit itatobvt taiyahli tuk osh,

265 miko: kamiti itvpeha mvto hatak itvnaha chito aiasha: yvmma fehnakma yakohmi hona nana isht vhlpisa tvli holisso atukmvno yakohmi hocha isht vlhpihisa hokvno—achit achukmalit anohonlashke—

266 Anumpa ma—il aiahlichit pin taiyaha hocha anumpa atukmvno pi hohchifo ha e lapalihinchishke

264 As for that. The Chief together with his committees have diligently decided on this legislation and finished making expenditures.

265 The Chief together with the committees and the main assembly have approved the funding for the policies that we have been making—this shall be well documented.

266 We have all agreed and finalized the law and therefore shall attach our names to it.

AUGUST 29, 1828

Iahokatvbi ×
Holvbi ×
Miashambi ×
Pistembi ×
Hakluntvbi ×
Koi humma ×
Hushishi humma ×
Jeremiah Folsom ×
PP Pitchlynn
Benjamin James
Robert Folsom

Lewi Folsom Ahepvtukla i miko vt aiokpvchit aiahlichi	Levi Folsom Chief of the Ahepvtukla approves
Imoklvsha Hopaii	Tribal Shamans
Pitema Hopaii Hopaii	Shamans
Hopaii Iskitini	

Index of Names

NOTE: The first letter of the Choctaw alphabet is *a* (the long *a*), and the second is *v* (the short *a*). Names in this index have been alphabetized accordingly.

Achintvbi, 65
Afamatvbi, 65
Aiushkemo, 65
Apuckshanubbee, 22, 23, 24, 34
Atvklvbi Tvshka, 63
Atonochvbi, 65

Baird, David, 4
Brashears, Jesse, 65
Brashears, Vaughan, 66

Chahta im ataha, 65
Chilahi humma, 65
Cobb, Samuel, 63
Cole, Robert, 23, 24
Comes, James, 65
Cushman, H. B., 10, 12, 22, 25

Debo, Angie, 4
Durant, Lewis, 65

Folsom, David, 22, 24, 25, 31; miko (Chief), 63, 67
Folsom, Israel, 21, 25, 71, 77, 79, 81
Folsom, Jeremiah, 65, 72, 77, 79, 81, 84, 91, 99, 105, 108, 113, 117, 121, 126, 129, 132, 135, 138, 144, 146, 150, 153
Folsom, Lewi, miko (Chief), 69, 72, 77, 80, 84, 91, 99, 105, 109, 114, 118, 121, 126, 130, 133, 135, 138, 144, 147, 150, 153
Folsom, Nathaniel, 22
Folsom, Robert, 65, 72, 77, 79, 81, 84, 91, 99, 105, 108, 113, 117, 121, 126, 129, 130, 135, 138, 144, 146, 150, 153
Folsom, Sophia, 4, 23, 29
Foster, Moses, 66
Foster, William, 66

Garland, John, 65
Garland, Samuel, 25

Hakluntvbi, 84, 90, 91, 105, 108, 113, 117, 121, 125, 129, 132, 135, 138, 144, 146, 150, 153
Hall, William, 65
Hargrett, Lester, 4
Hays, William, 65
Hvshi humma, 65
Hvshishimataha, 65
Hiopancho hvbi, 65

INDEX OF NAMES

Holvbi, Mecha (Major), 63, 69, 71, 77, 81, 84, 91, 98, 105, 108, 113, 117, 121, 125, 129, 132, 134, 138, 143, 146, 149, 153
Hopaii humma, 63
Hopaii iskitini, 63, 84, 91, 99, 106, 109, 114, 118, 121, 126, 130, 133, 135, 138, 144, 147, 150, 153
Hushishi humma, 84, 91, 99, 105, 108, 113, 117, 121, 125, 129, 132, 135, 138, 144, 146, 150, 153

Iacha Hopaii, 63
Iahokatvbi, Mecha (Major), 63, 69, 71, 77, 79, 81, 84, 90, 98, 105, 108, 113, 117, 121, 125, 129, 132, 134, 138, 143, 146, 149, 153
Iapalvbi, 65
Im oklvshi Hopaii, 84, 91, 99, 106, 109, 114, 118, 121, 126, 130, 133, 135, 138, 144, 147, 150, 153
Ishtanukahacho, 65
Isht imlhishi, 65
Isifoni, 65
Itinahalvbi, 65

James, Benjamin, 65, 84, 91, 99, 105, 108, 113, 117, 121, 126, 129, 132, 135, 138, 144, 146, 150, 153
James, Isaac, 65

Kvniohikvbi, 65
Kvpitvni Ohlehko, 65
Kvsh onahikat, 65
Kvsh ona holahta, 65
Kincaid, Joseph, 65
Kingsbury, Cyrus, 17, 28

Kisha humma, 65
Koi humma, 65, 84, 91, 99, 105, 108, 113, 117, 121, 125, 129, 132, 135, 138, 144, 146, 150, 153

Lauwintvbi, 65
LeFlore, Greenwood, 24, 25; miko (Chief), 63, 67
Lincecum, Gideon, 11, 12

McDonald, J. L., 66
Miashambi, 71, 77, 79, 81, 84, 90, 98, 105, 108, 113, 117, 121, 125, 129, 132, 134, 138, 143, 146, 149, 153
Miko hoyopa, 65
Mishamaia, 65
Mushulatubbee, 11–13, 21, 22, 24, 25, 30, 33, 34

Nail, Joel H., 65
Nvhlitvbi, 65, 72, 77, 79, 81
Nitakachi (Nittuckachie, Nitakechi, Nitakachi, Nittakachih), 23, 25
Nitak vbi, 65
Nitak echi (as Council member), 63

Ofi humma, 63
Ofi nowa, 65
Okinla, 65

Pahlinihvbi, 65
Pashi ishtikvbi, 65
Perry, Lewis, 63
Pickens, James, 65
Pisatvbi, 65

INDEX OF NAMES

Pistembi, 63, 71, 77, 79, 81, 90, 105, 108, 113, 117, 121, 125, 129, 132, 135, 138, 144, 146, 149, 153
Pitchlynn, John, 23, 29
Pitchlynn, Peter Perkins: early life, 29–31; as secretary of Council, 66, 84, 91, 99, 105, 108, 113, 117, 121, 126, 129, 132, 135, 138, 144, 146, 150, 153
Pitema Hopaii, 84, 91, 99, 106, 109, 114, 118, 121, 126, 130, 133, 135, 138, 144, 147, 150, 153
Pushmataha, 11, 12, 13, 22

Shapanvhahvbi, 65
Shvkha humma, 65
Shields, James, 65
Swanton, John, 7

Tahoka, 65
Tvnvpocha, 65
Tvpenahumma, miko (Chief), 63, 67
Tvshka holehta, 63, 65
Tecumseh, 11, 14
Tishu, 65
Tishu Miko, 63
Tuli humma, 65

Wade, William, 65
Wakachvbi, 65
Washashimastvbi, 63
Washington, John, 65
Weshakihi humma, 65
Willis, 65

Yukohlo Hopaii, 63

Index of Topics

ABCFM (American Board of Commissioners for Foreign Missions), report of, 4–7, 33
American Board schools, 25, 28, 31
Assault, 51–53, 106–108
Authorization of funds: for cotton manufacture, 70–71, 151; for council house, 67; excess funds, 151; for grounds for instruction, 69; for instructor, 149; for metalworking, 69–70, 151; for stray animal care, 122–25

Christian missionaries, 15, 17–18, 28
Committees, 51, 53, 59–60
Conflict between Mushulatubbee and Nittikachih, 25–27

Destruction of property, 56, 118–20
Disorderly conduct, 48, 74–75, 87–90. *See also* Assault; Killing
Distribution of annuities, 18–19, 25, 33–34

Early treaties, 14–17, 23, 24, 27

Fences, 114–16

Infanticide, 78
Inheritance, 91–98; intestate status, 93, 95; rights of relatives, 97; surviving children, 92, 95–96; widows/widowers, 93, 96; wills, 95–98. *See also* Marriage

Killing: accidental, 85, 87; of chief, 86; execution for, 89; incarceration for, 89; self-defense, 88; suicide, 87. *See also* Assault; Infanticide

Legal residence, 145–46
Lighthorsemen (lawmen), 72, 74–76, 90, 119–20, 128, 136–37
Livestock, destruction by, 114–16. *See also* Fences; Stray animals
Lying, 133–34

Marriage: bigamy, 104; between Choctaws and white men, 100–104; official status, 100–101; with slaves, 139. *See also* Inheritance
Mixed parentage leaders, 20, 22, 23, 34
Moieties, 10

INDEX OF TOPICS

Northeastern District, 11, 25, 27, 31

Origins myths, 7–8

Pardons, 82–83
Paying debt, 52, 54–55

Rape, 80, 127; false accusation, 127–28
Rules of the convention: correcting laws, 61; organization, 47; setting meetings, 47; speaking, 48–60; voting, 49

Selling land, 51
Selling possessions, 102–103
Six towns people, 8, 11
Slaves: prohibition on marriage, 139; sexual relations with, 140–43
Stealing: of animals, 72–73; inducing others, 130–32; petty, 73
Stray animals: care of, 109–13; liens on and reclamation, 122–25

White people, disputes with, 56. *See also* Marriage

www.ingramcontent.com/pod-product-compliance
Lightning Source LLC
Chambersburg PA
CBHW020935230426
43666CB00008B/1688